My Uncle Sam Needs a House Call

The Faltering Health of a Great Nation

by

Robert Poole, M.D.
The unabashed musings of a retired family doctor

Responsible liberty is our birthright. May it forever be our legacy.

ISBN: 1453642552

ISBN-13: 9781453642559

Library of Congress Control Number: 2010909159

Table of Contents

Preface v

Glossary ix

Section One—Understanding Health and the Patient 1

    Chapter I—Our Great Nation and How it Became So...................... 3

    Chapter II—Selective Memory 9

    Chapter III—Faltering Health?.. 15

    Chapter IV—What Seems to be the Problem? 21

    Chapter V—Wholeness is Dynamic 27

Section Two—Understanding the USA as a Patient 31

    Chapter VI—Pals, Polio, and Purpose.. 33

    Chapter VII—Healthful Beliefs 39

    Chapter VIII—A Social Projection of the Model 45

Section Three—A Tentative Diagnosis 49

    Chapter IX—The Illumination of Epidemiology.......................... 51

    Chapter X—A Tentative Diagnosis... 59

    Chapter XI—The Sterilization of Conscience?.............................. 65

    Chapter XII—Grace, Gratitude, and Greatness............................. 71

    Chapter XIII—The Dependency of Independence on Dependence........... 79

Section Four—Therapeutic Management 85

    Chapter XIV—Therapeutics 101 87

    Chapter XV—The Relief of Embarrassment 91

    Chapter XVI—The Relief of Adversarialism 107

    Chapter XVII—The Relief of Creeping Servitude 115

    Chapter XVIII—Definitive Therapy 125

    Chapter XIX—As a Matter of Fact… 137

Section Five—Preventive Medicine.. 143

    Chapter XX—A Stitch in Time Saves Nine 145

Section Six—Prognostic Variables and the Benefits of Care............ 151

    Chapter XXI—The Domestic and Global Benefits of

    Wholeness Rediscovered 153

    Chapter XXII—Ultimate Citizenship.. 161

Bibliography.. 169

Preface

This book is about the United States of America, my "sweet land of liberty," and I am writing it at the age of eighty. For reasons over which I had no control, I was born into a wonderful, functional family and into a nation structured to provide freedom and opportunity. For these reasons, I take no self-serving credit, nor do I make any apologies for references to personal experiences. That's what this book is all about—my observations!

I retired from the family practice of medicine in West Chester, Pennsylvania, in 1995 and have been living in White Horse Village, a Continuing Care Retirement Community (CCRC) located in Delaware County, Pennsylvania, since 2001. Most of the residents living here have interfaced with and knew personally five or six generations of family and friends. Consequently, we have been firsthand witnesses to an abundance of technological and sociological change. Citizens who have earned the modifier "senior" become progressively aware of the fact that our watches and calendars with leap year and millennial adjustments are but the feeble effort of humankind to reflect the remarkable precision of celestial events, a phenomenon called time. Our transient participation in that phenomenon is a reminder that we're each going to run out of that stuff called time, and this book may only be an expression of that realization.

West Chester is a culturally diverse community, and my family medical practice was immeasurably enriched by a corresponding reflection in its patient profile. Hence, my delivery of health care for more than forty years was an educational exercise in medical knowledge, sociological sensitivity, appreciation of age diversity, and cultural growth. My commencement from the Jefferson Medical College in 1953 was the commencement of learning in a very real sense. Now, I have always been discouraged by those who dwell on how things used to be. I can remember my mixture of amusement and resentment when my own parents commented critically on the subjects of zoot suits, DA (duck's ass) hairstyles, and two-piece bathing suits for girls. Personally I felt that zoot suits looked dumb, and I never could stand long hair. But as a healthy teenager with raging hormones, I thought that girls' two-piece bathing suits were the best thing since the invention of sliced bread (to use a worn cliché)!

Then, I found out that my parents had been lectured to by their parents about the potential social downside risk of the Charleston, whiskey, and the horseless carriage! To carry this story to a third generation of our lifetime, my wife, Anne, and I, with four daughters, found ourselves decrying miniskirts, the deterioration of the public school dress code, and the subsequent or consequent degeneration of juvenile behavior and scholastic performance.

Now we are listening to our children expressing concern to our grandchildren with regard to tattoos, body piercing, substance abuse, technologic indolence, and morbid obesity.

So, the beat goes on, and probably thus will ever be so. Ultimately, all who have been involved in intergenerational counseling no longer regard the process as "old fogeyism." The passage of time reveals that there are enduring values, and the desire to impart wisdom to the young is instinctive love at its best.

It is for these reasons that I refer to a concern about my Uncle Sam's health in this book's title. As a young nation, we are looked upon as a great nation. Is it possible for a great nation to slip away from the ideals that made it so? Is it possible that a review of those ideals might reset the sails in the best interest of those generations that follow? As a physician who knows a bit about symptoms, signs, diagnosis, and treatment, I submit these, my observations, for your consideration.

These observations are not offered as hope that things will go back to how they used to be. As an author with a wife and four daughters, I have great respect for the beauty and justice of women's rights. With good friends from other religions and races, I deplore the discriminatory prejudices of history. We have come a long way ethically, and as one who adores new knowledge, I am addicted to the comforts of air conditioning, the pleasures of television, and our huge strides in the use of the computer.

What I wish to recover is the best of the past. As a physician—a family physician, indeed, an older, retired family physician—I have learned that health in its fullest sense has quantitative and qualitative dimensions. The commercials of our day suggest that we have become a nation hysterically preoccupied with concerns relating to longevity. To be abundant, long life needs to be enriched with a personal sense of self-esteem, the joys of wholesome family relationships, and a sense of grateful humility. These truths were regarded to be self-evident by those who crafted our independence. We will be discussing the recovery of proud, unashamed, national patriotism, the community friendliness of bygone years, and the meaning of the liberty that was an intended feature of our republic.

When new friends discover that I am a retired family doctor, the amusing first question most commonly asked is, "Did you used to make house calls?" As a matter of fact and interest, I made them almost each day of my professional career. The decisive criterion was always whether the patient was too sick to come to the office—and those patients were most often the very young or the elderly. In those days, emergency rooms were for emergencies, and primary care physicians managed the unwell in the community accordingly. As a beneficial side effect, much of my practical sociological, psychological, economic, political, and religious postgraduate education was accomplished at the kitchen tables of diverse families in small-town America. Unconsciously, I was gaining an understanding of health in its fullest sense. It is in that context that I decided on the title of this book, *My Uncle Sam Needs a House Call.* Having witnessed the evolving erosion of wellness of the past fifty years, this physician is of the opinion that old Uncle Sam is too sick to come to the office!

My discussion of these matters necessarily involves the use of words. It has occurred to me that connotations sometimes differ for author and reader. For this reason I have called on our friend Noah Webster for a glossary to reflect my intended meaning. Perhaps a review of that glossary would best set the stage for this book and its purpose.

Glossary

Agnostic—One who holds the view that any ultimate reality, such as God, is unknowable.

Antinomianism—The rejection of socially established morality.

Atheist—One who denies the existence of God. Atheism is a disbelief in the existence of deity.

Belief—Conviction of the truth of some statement or reality when based on the examination of evidence (i.e., intellectual assent).

Bench research—Initial research performed in a laboratory prior to any clinical application.

Bias—An inclination of outlook; having an expected value different from others.

Common sense—Sound, prudent and unsophisticated judgement.

Conservative—One who adheres to traditional methods and views.

Corruption—Impairment of integrity, virtue, or moral principle.

Cytoplasm—The organized complex of inorganic and organic substances external to the nuclear membrane of a cell and including the cytosol and membrane-bound organelles (as mitochondria or chloroplasts).

Deduce—To infer from a general principle.

Determinism—A belief in predestination. A doctrine that social phenomena are causally determined by natural laws.

Disorder—A disturbance of the regular or normal functions.

Doxology—A liturgical expression of praise to God.

Dysfunctional—Impaired or abnormal functioning.

Epidemiology—A branch of medical science that deals with the incidence, distribution, and control of disease in a population.

Faith—Belief in something for which there is no proof. Belief in the traditional doctrine of a religion.

Faltering—Wavering and weakening.

Family—A people or group of peoples regarded as deriving from a common stock.

Glorification—To give praise, honor, and thanksgiving.

Goodness—Praiseworthy character. The nutritious, flavorful, and beneficial part of something.

Great—Markedly superior in character or quality.

Gross Domestic Product (GDP)—The market value of all final goods and services made within the borders of a country in a year.

Health—The condition of being sound in mind and body.

Hedonism—The doctrine that pleasure or happiness is the chief good in life.

Helix—A spiral formation.

Hope—To long for with expectation of attainment.

Humanism—A devotion to the humanities with an emphasis on secular concerns.

Humanist—One who rejects supernaturalism and stresses an individual's dignity, worth, and capacity for self-realization through reason.

Humanitarianism—A philosophy that usually rejects supernaturalism and stresses an individual's dignity and worth and capacity for self-realization through reason.

Human nature—The complex of fundamental dispositions and traits of human beings.

Induce—To determine understanding from particulars.

Knowledge—Facts or ideas acquired by study, investigation, observations, or experience. The sum of what is known; the body of truth, information, and the principles acquired by mankind.

Liberal—Not bound by authoritarianism, orthodoxy, or traditional forms.

Liberty—The quality or state of being free. The power of choice.

Marriage—The mutual relation of husband and wife.

Matrimony—The union of men and women as husband and wife.

Myth—A belief that embodies the ideals of a segment of society.

Normal/Norm—A pattern or trait taken to be typical in the behavior of a social group.

Pathology—The study of the essential nature of disease.

Personality—The complex of characteristics that distinguishes an individual or a nation or a group.

Philosophy—A search for a general understanding of values and reality by chiefly speculative rather than observational means.

Philosopher—One who seeks wisdom or enlightenment—a lover of knowledge.

Physiology—A branch of biology that deals with an organism's healthy or normal functioning.

Prejudicial—An irrational attitude of hostility directed against an individual, a group, or its supposed characteristic.

Rationalize—To provide plausible but untrue reasons for conduct.

Religion—The service and worship of God or the supernatural.

Republic—A government in which the supreme power resides in a body of citizens entitled to vote and is exercised by elected officers and representatives responsible to the citizens and governing according to law.

Ribosome—A protein-rich granule inside of a cell; site of protein synthesis.

Secularism—Indifference to or rejection of religion and religious considerations.

Serendipity—The faculty of finding valuable or agreeable things not sought for.

Skepticism—The doctrine that true knowledge or knowledge in a particular area is uncertain. Doubt concerning basic religious principles.

Superstition—A belief or practice resulting from ignorance, fear of the unknown, trust in magic, or a false conception of causation.

Truth—The property of being in accord with fact or reality.

Tolerance—A sympathy for beliefs or practices differing from one's own.

Unalienable—Incapable of being surrendered or transferred.

Wedlock—The institution whereby men and women are joined in a special kind of social and legal dependence for the purpose of founding and maintaining a family.

Section One

Understanding Health and the Patient

Chapter I

Our Great Nation and How it Became So

In spite of our many problems as a nation, the invitation from the Statue of Liberty (given by France in 1884 and named by the French *Liberty Enlightening the World*) continues to be the driving force behind U.S. immigration. That invitation was captured by the Jewish poet Emma Lazarus in words engraved on the statue's pedestal:

"Keep ancient lands your storied pomp,"

Cries she with silent lips.

"Give me your tired, your poor,

Your huddled masses yearning to breathe free,

The wretched refuse of your teeming shore.

Send these, the homeless, tempest-tost to me.

I lift my lamp beside the golden door."

That invitation brought my Poole paternal grandparents from Northern Ireland to settle on Cambria Street in North Philadelphia, while my maternal grandparents came from London (Bastin) and Germany (Kolbe) to settle in Doylestown, Pennsylvania. To this day I am the custodian of the Kolbe plot in the Doylestown cemetery, where my parents lie at rest, and where I periodically pause to remind myself of my roots.

For economic reasons, neither of my parents was able to complete a high school education. However, in this land of opportunity they impressed upon my older sister, my younger brother, and me our personal and sacred responsibility to develop any and all talents with which we had been blessed. It was in that context that educational pursuits, music lessons, and sports competition began.

As I look back to the 1930s, I strongly suspect that this emphasis on values and responsibility gave rise to my fondest grade-school memories of Memorial Day in Doylestown. The holiday always seemed to come on a warm, sunny day in May, after a long, gray winter. New life was bursting forth all around us, and we reported to our classrooms with armloads of peonies, lilacs, irises, and early roses. We were then led to the school playground to stand together as classes facing a platform stage that had been constructed for ceremonial purposes. I think that the beauty and overwhelming fragrance of those spring flowers may be responsible for the indelible mark made on my young memory.

On the platform behind the lectern sat a rather stern-looking clergyman, the mayor of Doylestown, the president judge of Bucks County, our American Legion commander, and the director of our high school band. The clergyman, usually the Rev. George Whitenack, Jr., pastor of the Doylestown Presbyterian Church, in his black suit and appropriate collar, led things off with an invocation that seemed endless. He often made comments about a Creator who comes to bring freedom to the oppressed. Pastor Whitenack's participation was usually followed by remarks from the mayor and the president judge about their derived powers in this government of, by, and for the people.

This Doylestown, PA K through 12 Public School building once stood on the corner of Broad and Court Streets directly across from the Melinda Cox Library in that beautiful community. Alumni of the school and patrons of the library include Margaret Mead (1918) and James Michener (1925). The original building, pictured on the right, was constructed in 1889. The entire school was demolished by fire in 1973. The multipurpose playground with its flagpole was the site of my own Memorial Day memories and is pictured during a May Day celebration, circa 1915. This community public school system has been replaced by the huge Central Bucks School District.

With the support of the high school band, we then sang the first and last verses of Kathryn Lee Bates' "America the Beautiful." Now, our family had never been further from Doylestown than Atlantic City, a three-hour drive. As a child, I had no feel for "amber waves of grain" or for "purple mountain majesties above the fruited plain," but later in life, when driving across the endless expanses of Kansas on camping trips with my own family, the stage had been set for my own special, personal appreciation.

Remarks from the legion commander, relating to the fact that freedom is not free, preceded the singing of "The Star-Spangled Banner" and then a four-block march behind the band to the Doylestown cemetery. There we placed our flowers on the flag-marked graves of "those who had given their last full measure of devotion" on our behalf. These exercises were terminated by the veterans' gun salute, as little boys scrambled at the feet of the riflemen to gather the ejected shells. That commotion was always followed by total silence, the quiet playing of "Taps" by a single bugler, and the muffled sobs from those who had lost loved ones.

Then it was back home to decorate floats and bicycles with red, white, and blue bunting for the town Memorial Day parade. The day always ended with the first swim and family picnic of the summer.

I don't know if this is what General John A. Logan had in mind when he established the holiday in 1868 following the Civil War. I do know that the events of the day gave interrelated meaning to a variety of values promoted by my folks—reverence, gratitude, natural beauty, music appreciation, education, patriotism, recreation, and family. As I look back, that interdependence of love for God and country defined patriotism through World War II and even during my own tour of duty in Korea with the United States Army between 1946 and 1948.

But the roots for the values captured in the celebration of Memorial Day were planted long before the Civil War. Carl Sandburg, in his biography of Abraham Lincoln (Volume I, page 35), described the first eight million European immigrants as "Puritans from England, French Huguenots, German Pietists, Hanoverians, Moravians, Saxons, Austrians, Swiss, Quakers, Scotch Presbyterians, and Ulster Presbyterians from North Ireland, all carrying their Bibles." Fifty thousand thieves and murderers were sent from British prisons and courts, and not included in the census count were one and one-half million slaves from Africa listed as property, not people.

From Bibles translated to their own language, these immigrants read about a God who valued each person equally, who came to deliver from bondage and to set at liberty all who were oppressed. Beyond deliverance from bondage to sin and fear of death, these folks came to escape civil totalitarianism in all forms, whether it be authoritarian, dictatorial, autocratic, theocratic, aristocratic, or monarchal.

It was upon that background that the colonists eventually declared their independence from England with the words, "We hold these truths to be self evident, that all men are created equal, that they are endowed by their Creator with certain unalienable Rights, that among these are Life, Liberty, and the pursuit of Happiness."

Twelve years later, in 1787, the same colonists penned a Constitution and Bill of Rights (1789) that would ensure the perpetuation of a government that would serve the people; a government of, by, and for them; a government that would forever respect the unalienable rights of its citizens. That amended and dynamic document has served the United States of America well for more than 220 years.

Yes, this is the great nation to which I was introduced by my loving parents eighty years ago—a nation founded on Christian hope, a nation imperfect from its birth, a nation perpetually striving to achieve the ideals of a Greater Kingdom, and a nation that pledged in the early 1950s to be "one nation under God." Kathryn Lee Bates had captured that work in progress when she wrote, "Oh beautiful for patriots' dream that sees beyond the years, thine alabaster cities gleam undimmed by human tears."

Chapter II

Selective Memory

It has been said with some degree of truth that "figures can lie, and liars can figure"—meaning that if given a bit of planning time, a rational argument can be constructed to support almost any conclusion.

Scholars tell me that this is particularly true of writings based on historical research. Much written history is not objectively accurate, inasmuch as it is inclined to reflect a point of view held by the author. In the late 1950s, I was chairman of the Intern Committee at the Chester County Hospital in West Chester. As a rural hospital, we had difficulty recruiting domestic medical school graduates and, of necessity, hired foreign medical graduates for house staff coverage.

To qualify for eventual licensure, many of these fine young people lacked the required undergraduate credits and thus would register for courses at the West Chester University. As an illustration of the contrasting historic perspectives, one of our interns had learned his American history from a French Jesuit priest in a colonial Central American country. That credential was unacceptable to our Board of Medical Licensure, and he signed up at our university for an American history course.

As one with the nonreluctant freedom to speak up, our intern proved to be a disruptive, yet constructive, member of the class. He had learned Civil War history from the French perspective and took great issue with the American textbook version. Indeed, the French, at political odds with the English who hoped for failure for this new young nation, sided with the North over issues of cotton and union preservation.

It has been called to my attention that my joyous account of Memorial Day in the 1930s is hardly a reflection of the mood of that moment. Didn't I know that the stock market had crashed in 1929? Didn't I know that my father was lucky to have a job during the Great Depression of the 1930s? Didn't I know that Adolf Hitler, a fanatical dictator in Germany from 1933 to 1945, was destroying the notion that World War I had been the war to end all wars? Didn't you know, doctor, that the 1930s were in the preantibiotic and pretechnologic era of health care—that disease was rampant, and that life expectancy was short?

Interestingly, I did know that my mother was providing lunch for homeless people on our back porch many days each week; and I did know about the argument of the isolationists that we should not get mixed up in the foreign affairs of other nations; and, with an abscessed knee and high fever and no definitive drugs, I did have a hallucinatory awareness of my family doctor sitting up at my bedside most of one night waiting for the "fever to break."

Nevertheless, my account of that era is from the perspective of a happy grade-school child in a loving, functional family in an idealistic Christian nation. That nation had adopted a motto in 1863, "In God We Trust," and we lived within that state of certainty. If we were poor, we were too happy to know it. Richness in values is priceless.

Meet Jean, Bobby and Teddy. I was raised with an older sister, Alice Jean, and a younger brother, Edward Otto. I was named for my father and grandfather, hence Robert Poole, III. Although our early years transpired during the Great Depression, our loving parents were attentive to the spiritual dimension of human nature...all other values fell into a natural order. The consequent strong sense of self-esteem was always associated with joy and a drive to serve humankind. We didn't know then that between us, with our spouses, we would beget thirteen (13) beautiful daughters. Talk about "cousins by the dozens".

As a physician, again as a completely fortuitous circumstance, I was privileged to practice medicine during an amazing interval in the art's history. During the late 1940s while in Korea, I was administering the new wonder drug, penicillin. In 1953 during my senior year at the Jefferson

Medical College, my professor of surgery, Dr. John Gibbon, used his invention, the heart and lung machine, to bypass the beating organ. That allowed him to arrest the contractions and, for the first time, to repair the inner parts of the heart under direct vision. Between 1950 and 2000, there had been a chemical and technological revolution in almost every specialty, with a consequent improvement in organic integrity and prolongation of life expectancy from less than forty years in 1900 to almost eighty years by century's end.

In 1998 I was invited to write about this remarkable medical era. The town of West Chester had been chartered in 1799. Consequently, in 1999, four years after my retirement, the bicentennial celebration was scheduled, big time. The town historian, Paul Rodebaugh, was asked to create a volume that would reflect the evolving changes during that two-hundred-year interval. Recognizing the magnitude of the assignment, Paul opted for a multiauthored book and invited me to write a chapter entitled "The Evolution of Health Care in West Chester, 1799–1999." Philadelphia was the center of health care for the colonies, and West Chester had grown up in the shadow of six medical schools.

1. The University of Pennsylvania, first in the nation, was chartered in 1765.

2. Then, on the other side of the Schuylkill River, the Jefferson Medical College opened in 1824.

3. The Female Medical College of Pennsylvania was chartered in 1850 and was renamed the Women's Medical College of Pennsylvania in 1910. Subsequently, with the admission of men in 1970, it was again renamed the Medical College of Pennsylvania.

4. The Hahneman Medical College was chartered in 1882.

5. The Philadelphia College of Osteopathic Medicine was founded in 1899.

6. The Temple Medical School of Temple University was founded in 1901.

With no background in writing, I accepted the invitation to study that two-century medical history, and, as is so often the case, learned more during the process of research than any reader of the future. In 1799 medicine was still laboring with the centuries-old presumption that disease was caused by extrinsic environmental vapors that would cause an imbalance between the body's four humors. Blood letting, as an effort to restore humoral balance, was an accepted medical method of the time, and there is still some speculation relating to the contribution of that practice to the death of our first president, George Washington (1732–1797).

The details of that two-hundred-year history are available under separate cover and are not of value for this discussion. Let it only be noted that we have moved from primitive notions, through a chemical understanding of physiology, to the precise chemical management of disease states. We have accomplished great advances in the field of noninvasive diagnostic imaging, and now, even organ transplantation. During the twenty-first century, many of the improvements in health care will be based on the knowledge of chromosomal derangements that are predisposing causes of many disease states.

With strides of this magnitude, it is my hope that your attention will be redirected to this book's title, *My Uncle Sam Needs a House Call*. Is such a title compatible with the claim that health care is better and life expectancy is longer than ever before in our world's history?

Chapter III

Faltering Health?

Understanding the "patient USA" during the last half of the twentieth century is so paradoxically ambiguous that this chapter will be more descriptive than analytical. On the one hand there was unparalleled, computer-implemented, technologic progress in almost every field of endeavor, a vast increase in wealth owing to real estate and investment appreciation, and a more liberal interpretation applied to our constitutional documents. On the other hand, in most of our communities, there appeared to be a decline in the stability of the nuclear family, deterioration of human behavior, an erosion of historic patriotism, and a drift in social mood akin to "malaise"—that is, a difficult-to-describe sense of ill-being. To make diagnoses, all medical students are trained to gather symptoms and signs, clues as it were, by allowing the patient to present a chief complaint and history of present illness, before conducting a physician-led systemic review to assure a thorough data search. Let this chapter represent that search in our diagnostic process.

Perhaps I should first explain that the joys of the golden years and the accomplishments of modern medicine are especially apparent to me at this time. You see, I had a total right-hip replacement at the Chester County Hospital ten days ago. The problem began with a painful limp on the golf course during the summer of 2007 and culminated with an x-ray that revealed a bone-on-bone absence of cushioning cartilage. My doctors are reasonably sure that they can deal with the limp but make no promises regarding the handicap, about which golfers have the greatest concern. I mention this event to assure you that I have now joined the ranks of the grateful and continue to marvel at the evolving medical and surgical accomplishments of my profession during the past fifty years.

In contrast to those marvels of today, let's get back to our medical history. As a young physician with a secure, trusting childhood, I was introduced to theft and vandalism by an experience that today seems humorous. One of my jealously guarded privileges as a family physician rested upon my right to come home for a quiet lunch. I did this one noon in the middle 1960s, when my wife was not home. As usual, I opened the garage door with my remote, pulled into the garage, gathered up my considerable load of paperwork with keys in gloved hands, and turned my hungry body toward the house door—only to find it locked! Oh, yes, now I remembered, because of a series of neighborhood daytime burglaries, my wife had decided on the installation of a home security system. Nevertheless, I could sense the heat of my angry red neck at having to unlock my own home. After dropping most of my papers while fumbling with gloves and keys, I finally got the door unlocked, only to be confronted by a shrill whistling sound. Oh, yes, now I remembered, I had sixty seconds to punch in four numbers to disarm the alarm system. I am sure that I had the numbers right, but no reordered combination of them stopped the whistle, and soon an inside-outside siren was screaming in my ears, and the dog was going crazy.

To my considerable relief, the sirens stopped after a wait that seemed endless, and I presumed that I was home free. However, as you can guess, when I slipped off my coat and reached for the refrigerator, the phone rang and a friendly lady from my security company wanted to know if I was aware of the triggered alarm. I assured her that I was, recounted for her the mistakes I had made, and reassured her that things were now well in hand. She politely wanted to know if I knew the "password"—what, to get into my own home? Well, yes, I did remember that my wife had selected the name of one of our previous pets to facilitate my memory. I went through a list of five or six cats and dogs and thought that I had finally established the right to have that quiet lunch in my own home. However, halfway through my sandwich, the doorbell rang, and there stood two serious-looking police officers with their hands on their sidearms. By this time I had moved from red neck to basket case, but humbly submitted to an identity check in the name of security. As I recall, I kissed man's best friend, my original receptionist that day, gave her the remains of my lunch, and took off to make house calls. I think that Rusty, our Irish setter, understood that you can't teach an old dog new tricks!

On a more serious note, during the interval under study, the Juvenile Probation Office in the Chester County Courthouse grew from three persons in 1955 to its present complement of more than forty full-time employees. Crime rates grew relentlessly, and overcrowded prisons demanding expansion were the rule nationwide. Divorce rates had risen to 50 percent of all marriages, with increasing numbers of single-parent homes and latchkey children. Teenage suicide had become commonplace. And now, our local, small-town newspaper is running a series of articles on the use of guns for defense in your own home. According to staff writer Jennifer Miller, "The use of a gun is but the final step in a series of efforts that homeowners should take to make sure that their homes are safe."

The strange contrast between longer life expectancy with newfound affluence and the decline in the social caring described by folks in all walks of life produced a puzzled population with poorly understood mood swings. But technically, we were up to the challenge, and a huge industry of mood-altering drugs was forthcoming—tranquilizers to calm anxiety and anti-depressants to combat sadness. The chemical alleviation of the negative emotions was the easy way out, for no one really understood the underlying stress of these times. The love of money was becoming more intense, the citizenry was becoming more litigious, and an unhealthy fear of the law reduced community voluntarism. White-collar crime soared, sports heroes cheated with performance-enhancing drugs, and all of the above increased insurance costs and the cost of living for everyone.

Hedonism, especially related to our God-given reproductive systems, seemed to surface as an overpowering force. As a normal physiologic drive, the contrast between male and female anatomy would seem to logically define sexual normalcy. However, arousal takes many forms, and some of those forms are socially destructive. The sexual abuse of children was and is of major concern to all healthy people, and in particular to young parents. Fear relating to the possibility of it has reached extremes.

In the late 1980s I invited my wife to go out for dinner, and, as one of the last of the big spenders, ended up at our local Boston Market Restaurant. As I sat down with my tray of food, I noted that a young mother had seated her preschool daughter next to us to hold the table, while Mom went through the line. Well, that sweet, little, blue-eyed blonde waved and smiled at me. She knew a vulnerable grandpop when she saw one, and I responded with friendly conversation. Just when things were going well, my wife prodded me with the admonition that continued conversation might get the child in trouble with her own mother.

After careful thought and subconscious resentment, I turned my face toward my platter and ignored my new little friend. Halfway through my mashed potatoes, I took a quick peek and discovered that the little lady had lost interest in me and was now engaged in animated conversation with a quite refined elderly woman sitting at the next table over. The child's mother finally returned, and everyone focused on food consumption. The elderly woman was the first to finish and, on her way to the door, commended the mother for having raised such a fine little girl. We were the next to finish, and as I passed my new little friend, I could hear her mother's words, "Yes, I know she looked like a good, kind, nice old lady—but how do you know? Please, don't talk to strangers." How sad! Young parents don't have any idea how things used to be.

It is understandable that wars do not always have the unqualified support of all citizens. However, the unpopular wars in Korea, Vietnam, and the Middle East were furthered by political exploitation on the home front, sometimes to the disadvantage of troops in harm's way and usually at the expense of patriotic instincts. Social fears and educational deficiencies undermined confidence in our public school system and gave rise to home schooling or vouchers for education in parochial and charter school settings.

The decade of the 1990s in our young nation's history was marred by the unfaithful sexual behavior of an elected president, who otherwise possessed tremendous potential as a world leader. That president was found guilty of lying under oath, was disbarred by his chosen profession, and has paradoxically survived with apparent popularity. This, and the misbehavior of many other elected officials, has led many from within the electorate to declare that "they don't represent us!" The greater fear, in light of public reaction, is that they *do* represent us, justifying my concern for this nation's faltering health.

Our sociological concerns are further intensified by the most recent *Pew Center Report on the States*. This factual report informs us that on January 1, 2008, 2,319,258 Americans were in prison. That happens to be one out of each 99.1 adults. This identifies the USA as the world's number one incarcerator. The national cost for corrections in 2007 was $49 billion…six times more than our spending for higher education. Add to these numbers the people on parole and bail, and the symptom of social misbehavior lends a critical dimension to our health concern!

This fifty-year interval was marked by new liberal meaning assigned to the wording of our constitutional documents. The new meaning related to the First Amendment's content requiring a separation of church and state. The new meaning from the Supreme Court has been used by some to try to suppress all religious expression from schools, courthouses, government buildings, and even currency. This movement for reinterpretation of the separation clause was led by the American Civil Liberties Union, representing groups offended by traditional and historic holidays and practices of the 1950s.

And to further muddy the waters during this fifty-year interval, what are we to make of the world's increasing disregard for American foreign policy, our domestic economic crisis of 2008, a U.S. dollar of decreasing value in the international economy, and the growing numbers of overt expressions of hate for the world's only surviving twentieth-century superpower? Is it possible that our faltering health is evident to other nations?

Again, my medical disappointment rests on the observation that people are living longer and enjoying it less. Others might say that my observations are sociological and that I should stick to health care. Nevertheless, we have an abundance of data relating to the last half of the twentieth century that is begging to be understood. To understate the complexity of the situation, we might ask the question, "What seems to be the problem?"

Chapter IV

What Seems to be the Problem?

During our young parent years, my wife and I discovered that a travel trailer and camping experience represented the best medium for enjoyable, educational, family-oriented, and, yes, inexpensive vacations. The trips covered most of the contiguous states and Canada, but six people in a twenty-two-foot, all-purpose room was not without its own sociological problems. "Mom, tell Tina to stop looking at me," or, "Dad, you barbequed the chicken into blackbird." Once, when we were stopped at the Canadian border, the customs officer, detecting turmoil generated by four daughters in the back seat, asked, "What seems to be the problem?"

That tagline became the wisecrack for many future family affairs and turned out to be the most important consideration of my professional life. In medicine we call it "diagnosis," and upon it all therapeutic decisions are dependent. "That child does not know what ails him," one of my grandmother's favorite expressions, has been discovered by me to be a clinical truth. Most patients don't know what ails them, and from the clues of symptoms and signs, diagnostic detective work is the real fun and the test of medical skill.

We indicated at the end of chapter 3 that societal concerns might be outside the so-called jurisdiction of the health care establishment of the twenty-first century. Common usage of the word "health" certainly suggests that to be so. If a physician's social greeting, "How are you?" is misinterpreted to be a medical question, he or she had better be ready for an organ recital!

Four hundred years before Christ, as in many primitive cultures, all human maladies were cared for by priests, who believed that illness was an expression of the anger of the gods. Hippocrates (460–377 BC), the father of modern medicine, showed that disease had natural causes that could be understood. He insisted that "our natures are the physicians of our diseases" and located his hospitals apart from the Greek temples of healing. He correctly identified medicine as a scientific art and separated concerns for organic integrity from care for a person's spiritual needs.

The explosion of knowledge in the early years of the twentieth century led to further fragmentation of patient care. Data evolving from the research of that day created problems for higher education, especially in the field of medicine. The solution and educational precedent for the century was offered by the Carnegie Foundation for the Advancement of Teaching in a report by Abraham Flexner, Ph.D., of Princeton University in 1910. Our undergraduate premedical, graduate medical, and postgraduate specialty training has evolved from that paper. Indeed, a medical credentialing process is now in place requiring board certification by peers in each specialty. This process is designed to assure high-quality patient care among residency-trained physicians and is envied by many professions.

The driving force behind health care excellence has always been human nature. All people in all cultures from the onset of recorded history have wished to live long and well. The demand for bright young people in research and patient care and the labor-intensive demands within the industry continue to reflect good health as a high human value. As additional evidence of our addiction to long life, it is of interest to note that beyond the approved measures of the Food and Drug Administration, the American public is spending a greater amount of money on alternative health care measures, which do not require approval by virtue of the Natural Substances Act of 1997, than it spends on physician-ordered remedies.

All of this discussion is intended to help us understand that the data load requiring specialization and subspecialization has caused fragmentation that detracts from an understanding of the person as a whole. "Wholeness" was an ancient Greek word that gave rise to the English word "health." Nevertheless, at this time in history no one can be all things to all people, and coordinated teamwork is the essence of today's patient care.

Doctors are aware of this problem. My wife recently had cataract removal with complex postoperative complications. Fortunately, the five-physician ophthalmology group had a person with subspecialty knowledge relating to each part of the eye. I expressed my admiration for the teamwork and the successful outcome, but the cataract surgeon exclaimed with a sigh, "Yes, but sometimes we have to remind ourselves that we're taking care of people."

Patients also are aware of this specialized detachment. I was speaking on the subject at Chapel Hill many years ago, and a rural family physician supported my observation with a firsthand account. He had sent a patient with vague face pain to the University of North Carolina for study. Several weeks later the physician was going over the extensive university report with the patient in his office.

The patient interrupted, "But Doc, I still have the face pain."

The doctor's immediate reply, "But Jake, didn't you see any doctors down there?" Jake responded, "I saw lots of doctors, but they didn't see me!"

As a matter of great interest to me, this fragmented consideration of people, started by Hippocrates twenty-four centuries ago, has recently been addressed by the leading geneticist of our day. Francis S. Collins, M.D., Ph.D, assumed leadership of the Human Genome Project of 1993, led more than two thousand scientists around the world to study the 3.1 billion gene sites on our forty-six chromosomes, and filed his complete sequencing report in April of 2003, the fiftieth anniversary of Watson and Crick's first description of the DNA double helix. Dr. Collins has been appointed by President Obama to head the National Institutes of Health in Bethesda, Maryland, where he now lives.

In his captivating book *The Language of God*, Dr. Collins describes the double helix as the nonprotein spiral ladder upon which DNA (deoxyribonucleic acid) is suspended—half from your mom and half from your dad. The genetic material contains a message from each parent, and, as such, we are true "chips off the old block." RNA (ribonucleic acid) is the messenger that transports that data to the cytoplasm of each cell, and, in obedience, the ribosome behaves chemically. This process is going on in each of the three hundred trillion cells that comprise the average human body—muscle, brain, liver, kidney, lung, ad infinitum.

As explained by Dr. Collins, "As a first approximation, one can therefore think of DNA as an instructional script, a software program, sitting in the nucleus of the cell. Its coding language has only four letters (or two bits, in computer terms) in its alphabet. A particular instruction, known as a gene, is made up of hundreds or thousands of letters of code. All of the elaborate functions of the cell, even in as complex an organism as ourselves, have to be directed by the order of the letters in this script."

Dr. Collins began his work as a professed atheist but was awestruck by the evidence of a Creator and a dimension of spirituality within the lives of those for whom his research was intended. Dr. Collins goes into great detail involving many fields of science but concludes convincingly that science and spirituality are complementary and not contradictory. He has done much to dismantle the 400 BC hurdle of Hippocrates.

The previous chapter, "Faltering Health?," suggests that our patient, the United States of America, has been undergoing a subtle personality change during the past sixty years. History suggests that our great republic was built on a great belief system. Does the perpetuation of our greatness depend on the cultivation of a direct connection between healthy beliefs and the way we act—inside and outside our borders? We need to be who we say we are and do what we say we'll do. Let it only be noted that health in its fullest sense involves all aspects of human nature. It is essential that we recapture the definition of "wholeness" if we are to ever comprehend "what the real problem is."

Chapter V

Wholeness is Dynamic

We spent the last chapter endeavoring to create a more comprehensive understanding of health using the word "wholeness." For the sake of clarity and understanding in the family practice of medicine, it is sometimes necessary to reduce the doctor's explanations to patients to similes involving pipes and pumps, wires and plugs, or oil and grit.

Plays on words run the risk of static concepts and an esoteric spin-off into the world of irrelevance. In this chapter let us explore "wholeness," and its faltering potential, as a dynamic process that comes through in everyday experiences, if you are a good listener.

Carolyn Doe was a very attractive young woman, a waitress in one of our community restaurants, the wife of a truck driver, and the mother of a four-year-old daughter and a two-year-old son, both delivered by me in the early 1960s. Carolyn called my office at 7:30 a.m., when my secretary first came on duty, and insisted that she see the doctor as soon as possible. She was given an appointment for 10:10 a.m. and was ushered into an examination room by my nurse to "wait for the doctor."

Nurse Sandy, a great little mother herself, had a keen sense for human behavior and suggested to me that Carolyn seemed like a different person that morning. "She thinks she's pregnant but seems overwhelmed with grief. Carolyn is a good mom. She really enjoyed her first two pregnancies, but this is very different."

I entered the examining room, and the patient, who was sobbing relentlessly, told me that she was pregnant, had significant lower abdominal discomfort, and had a horrible vaginal discharge. My secretary had allowed only the usual amount of time for the visit, but I too sensed its unusual nature. With that in mind, I picked up the intercom and asked Pat, my secretary, to reschedule two later morning appointments, and to ask Sandy to set Carolyn up for a pelvic examination.

Internal examination revealed no vaginal discharge, no pelvic pathology, and no evidence of pregnancy. This I expected would be the case. I helped the sobbing woman to sit up, explained the normal findings, and acknowledged the obvious: "But Carolyn, it is quite evident that you are very upset. What is that all about?" And then the story began to flow. "Oh, Dr. Poole, I am a terrible person, and I had to talk to someone." It was the case that while her husband was on the road, she had gone to a neighborhood party, imbibed to the point of modified inhibitions, and ended up in bed with her husband's best friend. "Dr. Poole, I couldn't tell my mother; she'd kill me. I couldn't tell my husband; he'd kill his best friend. I couldn't tell my priest; what would he think of me? And I'll bet you think I'm a terrible person, too!"

During this brief, commonplace, human encounter, it was evident that Carolyn had recruited significant courage to come to the office, felt better for having talked, and identified the role that she had hoped that I would play. Hey, they don't teach this stuff in medical school, but at times, family physicians are called upon to "wing it" in the best interest of patient care.

"Carolyn, as I see it, your problem is a sense of guilt. Your guilt relates to the human imperfection that affects each one of us. If you had gone to your priest, wouldn't he have told you that God has already forgiven you?" Carolyn acknowledged that Christian truth, but still felt that she had broken a promise.

"Well, Carolyn, your mom is not a factor in this situation, but your relationship with Tom probably does deserve some attention. Listen, you are a very attractive young woman, and I have great confidence in the power of the candle-lit dinner, honest confession, and consequent, sincere forgiveness at the human level. Why don't you farm out the kids to your mom some evening, prepare a quiet meal for Tom, tell him exactly what and how you told me, and in that context ask for his forgiveness?"

Some weeks later Carolyn, who was in my office for some other purpose, confessed to having taken my advice and had found out that on the road Tom had not always been an angel himself, and that by virtue of mutual forgiveness they were closer than ever before. I later delivered another child into that happy family.

My advice to Carolyn was replete with potential mishaps. It just happened to work well. However, there are many truths to be gleaned from that little everyday story, and I tell it to make the point that wholeness is a dynamic experience that is in action at all times. Carolyn came in with organic complaints that had been induced by an emotional upheaval relating to a sociological experience that conflicted with her religious convictions. All of those aspects of human nature are interacting synchronously; the process goes on twenty-four hours a day, and ultimately can shed light on human behavior—what makes people "tick," as it were.

Diagnostic skills often depend on simple listening to hear where the patient is coming from. Over the years I had unconsciously constructed a wholeness model that enabled me to trace the dynamic route of office conversations.

First of all, we are an organic entity with body systems that have been arbitrarily separated for purposes of research, teaching, and specialization. One of those systems is the central nervous system (CNS), which includes an organ called the brain—the seat of the mind and the personality. The CNS does many things, but above all it endows us with three major capacities that relate to human behavior. These three capacities include the ability to emote (feelings), the ability to relate to others (sociology), and the ability to believe. Hence my little model might take shape as follows:

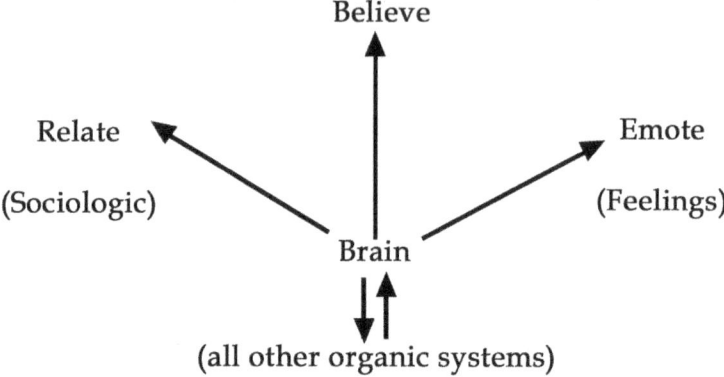

These capacities give us a feel for the objective ingredients of human behavior. However, to capture the dynamic, synchronous, and interrelated actions of all four components, indeed, to follow the story of Carolyn, we need many more arrows.

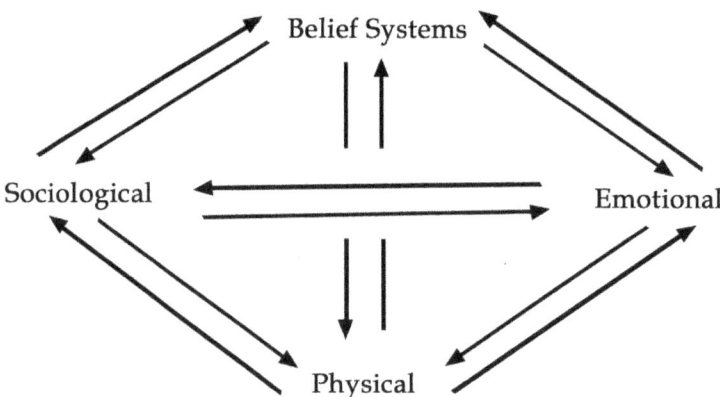

In a search for truth I have used Carolyn, a person, to comply with philosophical admonitions of years gone by, and those are "to know thyself" and "to thine own self be true." It is my hope that most readers will discover an element of personal relevance from my crude model.

Section Two

Understanding the USA as a Patient

☙❧

Chapter VI

Pals, Polio, and Purpose

I am sure that most of us, as we look back in our later years, can identify people or events that profoundly affected our own direction in life. In my own case, one such person turned out to be Clyde Custer Leaver, a second-grade friend I met when my family moved from Philadelphia to Doylestown in 1934. Clyde's father was a "gentleman farmer," and consequently Clyde always owned a pony. With a pony as the catalyst, we played together and often ate together at each other's homes, a friendship that continued even after his transfer to nearby Buckingham High School in the early 1940s because of World War II gasoline shortages.

These were preantibiotic and previral vaccine days, and swimming pools were closed parts of most summers because of poliomyelitis epidemics that would sweep across the nation. Consequently, during my freshman year in college in 1945, I was not totally surprised by a letter from my mother informing me that Clyde had contracted the disease.

Poliomyelitis is caused by a virus and is particularly cruel to children. Viral diseases are, for the most part, tissue specific and, for reasons not completely known, the polio virus usually attacks the spinal cord and brain stem. By damaging the central nervous system, the disease can paralyze muscles needed for leg use, arm activity, and breathing.

My mother's second letter indicated the disease had not only affected his legs but had caused a flaccid paralysis of both arms, prompting an admission to the Abington Hospital.

Her third letter reported an alarming spread to his brain stem with a paralytic arrest of his respiratory center and the need for iron lung ventilatory support. Clyde was on the critical list, with a poor prognosis for survival. In those days, 30 percent of polio patients would die, 50 percent were left with lifelong paralyses of varying degrees, and only 20 percent of the patients fully recovered.

After several weeks in the iron lung, Clyde's respiratory center did recover. He was removed from the "lung," but after many weeks of watchful waiting and rehabilitative efforts, it was evident that Clyde would never regain use of his arms or legs. However, the gray matter between his ears was completely unaffected, and Clyde's intelligence and personality remained intact. Understandably despondent, Clyde came face to face with so many questions we all ask about the meaning and fairness of life. And then, in the course of that struggle, an unforeseen human experience was in process. He fell in love with his student nurse, and she with him!

Now, Charlotte was a tall, slender, strong young woman—bright, intelligent, humorous, and fully aware that she would become a lifelong twenty-four-hour-a-day private-duty nurse, homemaker, and chauffeur. She probably would be a little angry if she knew that I described her in that fashion. She regarded herself as a faithful wife, homemaker, and mother! Yes, Clyde's autonomic nervous system was in perfect working order, and the devoted couple became parents of a daughter and a son.

Clyde told me later in life that my parents had played a significant role in his emotional recovery. During our childhood Clyde often ate at my home, where giving thanks before eating was the rule. He was always impressed by the reverence and sense of joyous gratitude evoked by that practice.

During his despondency, when all else failed, Clyde developed a faith of his own. He studied scripture, taught children in church school, and became an elected leader in his congregation. It was amazing to me to see Clyde living a life truly filled with love, hope, purpose, and happiness, when human logic would have predicted an existence of hopelessness, worthlessness, and depression. His life gave meaning to my own youthful theology—practical benefits in the here and now.

Clyde's restored self-image created ambitious undertakings of unimaginable proportions. With a stick inserted into the center hole of a Tinkertoy wheel, a rubber eraser on the end of the stick, and a straight pin inserted through the eraser, Clyde created a mouth-held tool that enabled him to type, open and close file drawers, flick through file cards, and effectively move cards end over end into his typewriter to accomplish correspondence. With those skills he developed a stationery and greeting card business to support the family.

The technological advances of the last half-century opened more doors, and he traded the electric typewriter for a computer and printer while that industry was in its early stages. Then, to improve self and family, he studied the investment industry and became a successful stockbroker. When I retired in 1995, he told me that he was unable to do so, because so many older folks were depending on him for economic advice.

Socially, Clyde and Charlotte were a delight. They traveled together, and in fine restaurants she got him in and out, cut and fed him his ordered meal, anticipated his every need, and participated in table conversation with candor and humor. All was so normal and spontaneous that Clyde's limitations were almost unnoticeable.

Because of his idealism, Clyde then developed a concern for the sociological deterioration of those days now addressed by this book. In spite of his full plate, he ran for public office and was elected a Bucks County district judge. Upon successful election, his business office doubled as a courtroom, and Charlotte's duties were expanded to include gowning the judge and wheeling him into his chambers at all hours of the day and night, where he would lecture to miscreants regarding their social irresponsibility.

Unfortunately, my good friend passed away in the late 1990s after fifty years of productive living as a quadriplegic. Charlotte died a few years later. I tell their story in the context of this book for several reasons. In spite of catastrophic disability that might spawn hopelessness and cynicism, Clyde and Charlotte acquired a belief system that provided purpose, hope, and happiness. Secondly, Clyde's story illustrates the unlimited opportunity offered by this great nation for those with a sense of self-worth. Third, Clyde's experience, plus the accomplishments of many other patients in my practice, has left me with a new and boundless understanding of the human spirit and its ability to rise above misfortune. And last but not least, Clyde's heroism during our nation's interval of faltering health was an inspiration to me. To count him and Charlotte as good friends for all those years has been a priceless blessing for Anne and me.

Now how does the story of a great friend relate to a great nation searching for meaning? Bertrand Russell, a confessed atheist, made the interesting observation that "unless you assume a god, the question of life's purpose is meaningless." Rick Warren points out in his best seller, *The Purpose Driven Life*, the discovery of identity is key to the understanding of purpose. The power of my friend Clyde's witness is best captured in this poem of Russell Kelfer:

You are who you are for a reason,
You're part of an intricate plan.
You're a precious and perfect unique design
Called God's special woman or man.

You look like you look for a reason,
Our God made no mistake.
He knit you together within the womb,
You're just what he wanted to make.

The parents you had were the ones he chose,
And no matter how you may feel,
They were custom-designed with God's plan in mind
And they bear the Master's seal.

No, that trauma you faced was not easy,
And God wept that it hurt you so.
But it was allowed to shape your heart
So that into His likeness you'd grow.

You are who you are for a reason,
You've been formed by the Master's rod.
You are who you are, beloved,
Because there is a God.

Pictured here is the first grade class of the Doylestown Public School in 1932. This nucleus of "town kids" was joined in our high school grades by wonderful "farm kids" bused in from surrounding rural areas. As a "townie", I walked to and from school each day in all seasons. Clyde Leaver is the little guy third from the right in the front standing row. During our twelve memorable years we had solid families, dedicated and capable teachers, fine teams for all sports, and a close working relationship between parents and teachers. We did not have a disrespectful relationship between genders, problems of substance abuse, destructive patterns of social behavior or "troubled children" in need of special attention. Sixty-five years later this Class of 1945 met in the fall of 2010 to celebrate those fond memories and enduring friendships.

❖ ❖ ❖

Chapter VII

Healthful Beliefs

As a physician writing a book that is health oriented, I confront this as my most arduous chapter. I have no formal educational background in theology and suspect that this discussion might lead me dangerously close to subject matter about which others are much more knowledgeable.

Perhaps you will find my observations to be more related to the theological implications of the here and now. In my later years I have come to call that "medical theology" and have consequently titled this chapter "Healthful Beliefs." I am less interested in ritual and ceremony and more interested in the practical, relevant, everyday manner in which personal beliefs find expression, where the "rubber meets the road," as it were (another trite, well-worn expression).

My favorite Old Testament prophet was Micah, who suggested that God is less interested in ceremonies and sacrifices, and more hopeful that all people will love mercy, do justice, and walk humbly with Him in matters of worship. It has been wisely noted that practical living involves both scripture and newspapers. Scripture alone risks the cultivation of a pious recluse. Newspapers alone tend to create a person who is cynically despondent.

In my human-nature model, I have labeled belief systems as one of the forces at work affecting Carolyn's previously described behavior concerning her unfaithfulness. I sometimes think that in addition to a higher level of intelligence, the capacity to believe distinguishes *Homo sapiens* from all other living species. After all, animals of many species emote and socialize. Considered objectively, believing is something that we all do, consciously or subconsciously.

In my experience, the process of belief for all people usually begins as simple philosophic speculation or wonder. Questions such as, "In light of the order I see all around me, the precision of celestial events, the functional complexity of the human body, I wonder if a Creator exists?" Or, "In the context of the vastness of the universe, I wonder if I have any significant value?" Or, "Is life just an experience defined by birth and death, or does it have meaning with an eternal dimension?" People have wondered in this fashion for centuries, and, as a matter of fact, such speculation is a very real part of human nature.

Beyond such speculation lies the human fact of hope—hope that the answers to these questions are affirmative. As human beings, most of us hope that there is a loving Creator God, that history is unfolding in accordance with His will, and that in His eyes we are people of worth. As created human beings, most hope that because of a soul, there is an eternal dimension to personhood. That's what funerals are all about.

After conceptualizing and hoping that God exists, the third step in the creation of our belief system is the expression of voluntary, intellectual assent; that is, belief in that for which we hope. Conversely, as agents with free will, we may elect to believe that God does not exist. Cultivation of an affirmative decision and the consequent confidence in those things hoped for is referred to as spiritual growth or faith. This aspect of human nature impacts the emotional and sociological life of the individual with great force, directly affecting behavior and consequently deserving special health-related attention.

Historically, we have paid much attention to the physical, emotional, and sociological aspects of our health model; but because of its long separation from our understanding of health, we have paid little attention to the integrity of belief systems. We must draw that concern back into the concept of wholeness, search out those practices and beliefs that have detrimental effects on health, and emphasize those that are healthful.

As a matter of interest, by virtue of the greatness of this nation, I can count among my dearest friends people who have liberal and conservative persuasions relating to Protestant, Roman Catholic, Jewish, and other religions. We respect the birthright origins of our differences, the social value of our respective beliefs, and our mysterious siblinghood as children of God.

Beyond that, I have had some international experiences to arouse my own curiosity. As a member of the Rotary Club of West Chester, I was elected to represent the fifty clubs in Southeastern Pennsylvania in 1980, a position called district governor. The International Convention was held in Rome that year, and my wife and I enjoyed a wonderful trip to Italy. Although my main interest was in sightseeing, I did want to hear a featured speaker at a downtown luncheon. Rather than fight the traffic, I left my wife and the rental car at our hotel and elected to use the public transportation of that beautiful city—big mistake! Although I had left the hotel with plenty of time to spare, I arrived at the restaurant forty-five minutes late and was ushered through a packed dining room, past the head table, through a steamy kitchen, and into a back room equipped with a very poor, unintelligible speaker system. After studying my lap during an interval of self-pity, I looked up and was encouraged to see a bottle of wine just beyond my water glass. Just beyond the wine bottle sat another late arrival, who turned out to be Yoshitaka Tsukamoto, a ninety-some-year-old past district governor (1969–70) from Rotary District 266 in Osaka, Japan. He had come approximately the same distance from the other side of the world to hear the same speaker, and, fortunately, spoke better English than I did Japanese.

We both began to laugh at the hopelessness of our situation and mutually agreed that only through conversation might wasted time be converted into meaningful experience. He set the stage by offering to describe Rotary in that part of the world. I responded to the effect that my understanding of service club work relates to my own Judeo-Christian upbringing. Back then, some of the most generous Rotarians in the world were from Japan, and I was curious about the motivation behind that level of commitment.

He smiled knowingly from behind his thick glasses and said, "Bob (we were first-name-basis Rotarians by then), you have heard it said that 'he profits most who serves best.' " This was an old motto used by Rotary in its early years, and I acknowledged having heard it many times. Then he said, "We really believe that." He then embarked on a long, possibly Buddhist, philosophical explanation about the achievement of inner peace by helping less-fortunate brothers and sisters on this planet Earth.

I thought that I had just heard an Oriental version of Christ's Sermon on the Mount and was again reminded of the many practical common denominators to be discovered in the world of healthful beliefs. At the end of the Rotary speech, which neither of us heard, he bowed formally from the other side of the empty wine bottle, and I reached down to the little man, in my clumsy Western way, and embraced him. We both understood, as we parted ways, that we had each grown a little.

Once again, as a layperson, I find that most of us folks want to understand why we believe what we believe. We are sincerely interested in the here-and-now implications of a sound belief system and find the third step of the faith journey, that is, intellectual assent, to be less of a stumbling block if we understand beliefs in the context of health.

My more than forty years in the practice of family medicine leads me to believe that each of us possesses a belief system that participates mightily in our behavior and demeanor. That belief system can have healthy and unhealthy features, as can the soma, or the physical self. Having used Carolyn and Clyde to illustrate that simplistic model, can the collective behavior and misbehavior of this great nation be similarly rationalized?

Chapter VIII

A Social Projection of the Model

During our discussion of Carolyn's commonplace human predicament, we were able to identify the behavioral forces of emotion, human relationships, and conscience. As described, these modifiers are at work synchronously within each of us at all times. The question being addressed in this chapter relates to collective national behavior. Can the individual personal model be imposed with validity on a societal unit to accomplish behavioral understanding? In a very basic sense, the institutions of society are historically a reflection of human nature. We have health care facilities because health sometimes fails; we have educational institutions because we love to learn; we have financial institutions because we have economic needs; we have industry because of our bent for creativity and vocation; and we have places for worship because of that interesting dimension to our nature.

It should be obvious that group considerations inevitably involve diversity. This is especially true of the powerful force of belief systems. We have the issues of comparative religions and, within each religion, degrees of commitment that range from atheistic rejection to agnosticism to all varieties of skepticism to absolute belief.

I once had a patient ask me, "Doc, what's your take on this God business?" The answer to that question could be to offer a discourse on what I think he wants to hear, to tell him it's none of his business, or to honestly relate my version of medical theology. He didn't wait, however, and succinctly said, "Personally, I'm going to keep up my church membership and attend on Christmas and Easter, just in case there's anything to it!"

In spite of such a wide spectrum of religious commitment, nations develop labels, and it is understood by all that labels do not imply uniformity. Labels more commonly reflect historic influences and population majority representation. India has a remarkably diverse population but is still referred to as a Hindu nation. Russia celebrated one thousand years as a Christian nation in 1988, in spite of its collapse as the Soviet Union, decades of Communist-forbidden religious practice, and tsarist disregard for human rights.

In a similar fashion, the United States of America has been known as a Christian nation in spite of its "melting pot" reputation for unparalleled diversity. That label relates to the historic facts about the first wave of immigrants, the influence of their Christian belief on the Declaration of Independence and Constitution, and the continuing influence of a religious majority in matters of civil government and politics.

The most recent study by the Pew Forum on Religion and Public Life reveals that 78 percent of the U.S. citizenry identify themselves as Christian, 1.7 percent as Jewish, 4 percent as atheist, less than 1 percent as Muslim, less than 1 percent as Buddhist, and 12 percent as unaffiliated. Roger Finke, a Penn State University sociological participant in the survey, states, "In the past, certain religions had a real holding power from generation to generation, but right now, there is a dropping confidence in organized religion, especially in the traditional forms."

It is of interest to note that it was Christian insistence that resulted in the constitutional prohibition of an official state religion. Freedom to believe, not to believe, and to worship or not worship have been constitutional guarantees since 1789. The downside of theocracy had been well demonstrated historically. It is hoped for by few in this great nation to this very day. Nevertheless, the model of wholeness developed during our discussion of Carolyn can be justifiably imposed on the sociological unit known as the United States of America. In spite of the nation's many flaws, biblical religious liberty was translated into national revolutionary independence, and a nontheocratic United States government was designed to serve the citizenry.

Many immigrants still come to this country in response to the benefits of liberty and opportunity. Those benefits still relate to the scriptural truths that provide civil experiences unheard of in the "old country." Once in the fold, all newcomers develop a common allegiance to a nation that provides an ethic with sociological and emotional benefits for the voluntary taking. That ethic is factually and historically rooted in Christianity and affords the stability of our rule of law.

The beauty of the wholeness model lies in the fact that it can be projected upon domestic and even international religious diversity in a nonjudgmental fashion. Are religious concepts that compromise human rights because of race or gender healthful? Can religious scripture of any kind that encourages suicide or murder of others be regarded as sociologically healthful? Does religion intensify guilt and depression, or, in the name of wholeness, should it promote a personal sense of forgiveness and behavioral betterment? Such questions can be addressed rationally, and strengthened belief systems are the consequence.

To assure domestic fairness and international harmony, every nation needs a healthy conscience. Unfortunately, the constitutional reinterpretation between 1950 and now has constructed an unintended barricade between church and state that tends to reduce spontaneous, meaningful interaction. In classrooms, courtrooms, chambers of commerce, and town councils, we are so focused on political correctness that deliberations become exercises in nervous, sterile secularism.

We still carry the label "Christian nation," but since 1950 deterioration of domestic behavior and international respect suggests that much meaning relating to that label has been lost.

Section Three

A Tentative Diagnosis

Chapter IX

The Illumination of Epidemiology

Much of the medical progress during the past two hundred years has been the result of the profession's scientific attention to the discipline of epidemiology. A great deal of understanding and truth can be gained by studying facts of the past pertaining to geographic, racial, seasonal, and age-related matters of disease incidence and distribution. The relationship between summertime, swimming pools, and children was known long before the polio virus was ever isolated. The relationship between irradiation and cancer was observed among watchmakers who painted the numbers with radium to facilitate time reading in the dark. It has been said that "those who fail to learn from the mistakes of history are doomed to repeat them." Is it possible that history could shed light on an abundance of miscellaneous symptoms that suggest the faltering health of a sociological unit?

For your consideration I would like to share the observations of Arnold J. Toynbee (1889–1975), a British historian who wrote *A Study of History*. This twelve-volume analysis of history from a global perspective examines the rise and fall of civilizations—a flowering and decline based on universal rhythms. He was, in effect, a sociological epidemiologist endeavoring to accomplish understanding by identifying the common forces that contribute to faltering health, decline, and demise.

In the light of our expanded understanding of wholeness, it can truly be said that sociological bondage is unnatural and unhealthy. As colonial slave owners, we paradoxically identified ourselves in our Declaration of Independence as creatures of a Creator who endowed each of us with the unalienable human right of liberty. This paradox was addressed by the most violent war to ever befall our nation, the Civil War. As a student of history, it always fascinated me that Washington, the capital of the North, was but a few miles from Richmond, the capital of the South. In 1864, when the violent hostility was winding down, our president, Abraham Lincoln, traveled down the Potomac River, into the Chesapeake Bay, up the James River, and anchored near General Grant's headquarters. We have much to learn again from the fine little book of Anthony Gross titled *The Wit and Wisdom of Abraham Lincoln*: " 'I want to see Richmond,' Lincoln said, when he heard that that stronghold was once more in Union hands. He went by river from Grant's headquarters and landed from a twelve-oared barge near Libby Prison. No military escort to meet him, and not even a vehicle of any kind. Taking his boy Tad by the hand, he walked through the streets for a mile and a half, guarded only by ten sailors. The negroes were wild with joy when they beheld their emancipator, before whom they prostrated themselves. 'Don't kneel to me; that is not right,' he said; and a leader among them commanded in a hoarse whisper, ' 'Sh—'sh—be still; heah our Saviour speak.' Lincoln said: 'You must kneel to God only. I am but God's humble instrument, but you may rest assured that as long as I live no one shall put a shackle on your limbs. God bless you, and let me pass on,' he said to them, as he passed along. Again in the strange progress of this modest conqueror an old slave lifted his hat, and the President returned the salutation by lifting his, whereat the crowd of negroes who followed him gaped in wonder to see a white man uncover to a black. We are told that the emancipated slaves pressed around him, kissed his hands and his garments, shouted and danced with joy, while tears ran down the President's care-furrowed cheeks."

Liberty from bondage is an instinctual manifestation of personal and social health, and that bondage can be to powers of addiction, habits of behavior, or, in its variety of forms, social injustice. With a Revolutionary War memory of bondage to England and slavery as part of our own nation's history, let us turn to Toynbee's *Study of History* to learn more about that despised, sad condition

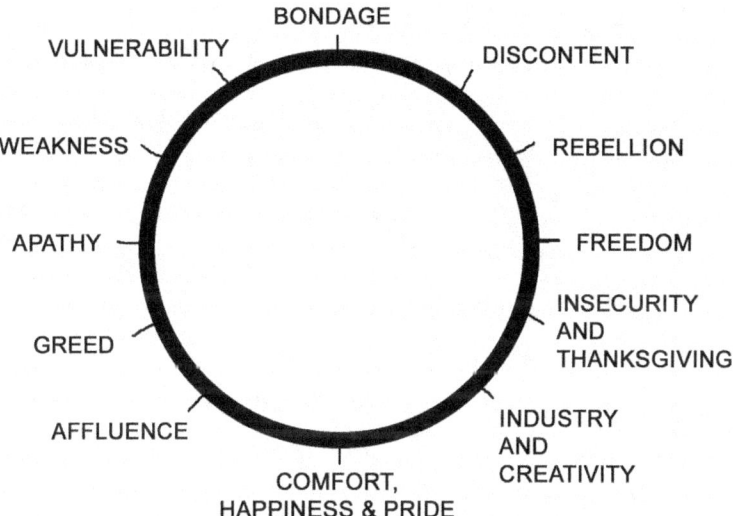

Throughout human history students have described the rise and fall of nations and civilizations in accordance with the above-diagrammed pattern. It is human nature to resent bondage, a difficult struggle to achieve freedom, and an exercise in grateful happiness to work toward security. Too often the social unit then forgets the sacrifices of those who have gone before; allows the legacy of patriotic comfort to be displaced by affluence, greed and apathy; only to return to the weakness and vulnerability that precedes the loss of liberty. Arnold Toynbee is of the opinion that this cycle is commonplace but not inevitable.

Toynbee writes, "Why have some civilizations broken down in the past? I do not believe that civilizations are fated to break down, so I begin by exposing the fallacious arguments of the determinists. I ascribe the failure of creativeness and growth to the spiritual demoralization to which we human beings seem to be prone on the morrow of great achievements—a demoralization to which we are not bound to succumb, and for which we ourselves therefore bear the responsibility. Success seems to make us lazy, self-satisfied or conceited. The civilizations that have already died are not 'dead by fate'; and therefore, a living civilization such as the Western Civilization is not doomed inexorably in advance *migrare ad plures:* to join the majority of its kind that have already suffered shipwreck. The divine spark of creative power is instinct in ourselves; and, if we have the grace to kindle it into flame, then 'the stars in their courses' cannot defeat our efforts to attain the good of human endeavors."

In his study of comparative history, Mr. Toynbee examines Egyptian, Hellenic, Roman, Sumerian, Eastern Orthodox, Germanic, Western, and other civilizations, and concludes that they die from suicide, not by murder. For Toynbee, civilizations are not intangible or unalterable machines, but a network of social relationships within their borders and, therefore, subject to both the wise and unwise decisions they make.

Toynbee recognizes that all people are created with intrinsic, equal worth but vary in identity. Some are blessed with talent in music, art, economics, teaching, scholarship, engineering, and on and on—and thank goodness we do differ. Mr. Toynbee observes that throughout the civilization cycle, gifted leaders have arisen from within the social body and have become, as a creative minority, the leaders of the day in their own areas of expertise. He calls them collectively the dominant minority. During the first half of the civilization cycle, from bondage to happiness and pride, the gifted leaders are bound patriotically to the masses from whence they came by the common goals of the entire social unit—the accomplishment of identity, strength, comfort, and happiness.

In his chapters on civilization decline and collapse, however, he describes the development of vertical and horizontal schisms. Within the minority leadership in times of affluence, leaders evolve that are no longer motivated by the idealistic struggles of bygone days. Creativeness is replaced by the greedy desire to capitalize on the society's successes. And, unfortunately, the masses are tempted to follow that hedonistic invitation.

But Mr. Toynbee digs more deeply and identifies "schisms" as only a superficial manifestation of an etiologic force that he identifies as "spiritual demoralization." Both he and Bertrand Russell have observed the fact that when times are tough, people are more attentive to their belief systems. When times of ease and affluence dominate the mentality of the group, the strength of self-discipline is threatened by the love of pleasure, creativeness is destroyed by antinomianism, social harmony by social discord, and peace of mind by spiritual "malaise." I was surprised to discover the use of that word "malaise" by Mr. Toynbee in his brilliant discourse.

In his chapter titled "Challenge of Disintegration," Mr. Toynbee emphasizes that evil is within and therefore subject to will. He is of the opinion that the key to cosmic unity rests in the love and law of ultimate spirituality that overcomes self-centeredness. In his words, "We must see beyond preoccupation with the mundane to the supra-mundane of a spiritual order." That can only result from a human resignation to endeavor by the arduous effort of will.

In faltering times, that change of direction, according to Mr. Toynbee, is dependent on the emergence of a strong, new creative minority from within the proletariat (or body politic). Even in the presence of unparalleled affluence, strong, patriotic, healthy leaders from the worlds of business, music, art, law, health care, entertainment, education, and religion can restore an apathetic social unit to a state of growth, happiness, and world leadership.

But the epidemiological observations of an idealistic historian are sterile without the expenditure of our effort at contemporary application. After all, the survival of the republic was doubted by many at the moment of its conception. Alexander Tyler, a Scotsman, commented on this new nation in 1775: "A democracy cannot exist as a permanent form of government. It can only exist until the voters discover that they can vote themselves largesse from the public treasury. From that moment on, the majority always votes for the candidates promising them the most benefits from that public treasury with the result that a democracy always collapses over a loss of fiscal responsibility, always followed by a dictatorship. The average of the world's great civilizations before they decline has been two hundred years. These nations have progressed in this sequence: From bondage to spiritual faith; from spiritual faith to great courage; from courage to liberty; from liberty to abundance; from abundance to selfishness; from selfishness to complacency; from complacency to apathy; from apathy to dependence; and from dependence back again to bondage."

To accomplish relevant application, is it possible to superimpose the two hundred and thirty-three year history of our great nation upon this civilization cycle that has been described by so many? Is it fair to identify the year 1776 as our moment of accomplished freedom? Do we see the bondage, discontent, and rebellion in the centuries of settlement preceding the Revolutionary War? Do we remember the grateful insecurity, industry, creativity, happiness, and proud patriotism of the struggling generations between 1776 and 1976? And can we identify with the subtly intensifying affluence, greed, irreverence, and pleasure seeking that have characterized the past fifty years?

If, indeed, we can see ourselves following the trail to "shipwreck" as blazed by so many preceding civilizations, we are assured by Mr. Toynbee that by virtue of free will, Western civilization is not inexorably doomed. It is within the power of a great nation to regain the spiritual creativity upon which it relied during its struggling years and rise to heights not yet envisioned. The power of that spiritual creativity was captured in the Declaration of Independence with the most important words ever penned in a nation's history: "We hold these truths to be self evident, that all men are created equal, that they are endowed by their Creator with certain unalienable rights, that among these are life, liberty, and the pursuit of happiness."

Thomas Jefferson did not go into the details of Judeo-Christian theology, the Gutenberg and Reformation facts of European history, the Magna Carta and parliamentary governmental evolution of our British background, or even the French, secular, revolutionary writings of Voltaire. He simply stated that the thirteen British colonies were populated by immigrants who "hold these truths to be self evident." Holding truths to be self-evident is a statement of belief and immediately identified those colonists and a hoped-for new nation as a community of believers. What were those truths believed to be self-evident?

The first truth—that all men are "created"—was a statement of common human belief. As far as we know, the capacity to believe such things is unique to the human species, and, as a fact, the statement was not challenged by the Continental Congress. The second truth—that "all men are created equal"—was a powerful statement to all monarchs, aristocrats, dictators, and others who might claim intrinsic superiority. To all people to this very day, this truth provides the motivational force of human dignity and self-esteem. It also opened the door of opportunity to all for the joy of fulfillment.

The third truth—that this Creator has endowed each human being with an "unalienable right to life, liberty, and the pursuit of happiness"— provided healthy hope for this new, fragile, political entity called the USA. This thirty-some-word statement shaped the construction of the Constitution and Bill of Rights more than a decade later, the termination of slavery by civil war, and the recognition of the full and valued potential of women. This statement of identity continues to evolve and harmonize with the hopes of humankind, as rates of U.S. immigration continue to exceed those of every other nation. We became great, indeed, because we believed that people have worth, that life has a purpose, and that history has meaning.

Our exploration of historic epidemiology has been factually productive. The defining opening statement of our Declaration of Independence clearly identifies a Creator and His good gifts of human rights as the strong foundation for this new republic. Similarly, it is a matter of fact that for the first ten generations of citizens who have populated our first two hundred years, the spiritual creativity of that belief system has produced a standard of living and an idealistic civilization of hope that is still in process. Factual consideration of civilized history further suggests that the United States of America is right on schedule for the emergence of affluence and the unfortunate temptation of greed.

How refreshing it is to be reminded by Mr. Toynbee that we are, by fact, agents of free choice. Apathetic greed need not lead to an inevitable return to bondage if the spark of spiritual creativity is rekindled. There is such a thing as a state of healthy affluence. It is apparent to me that this moment in history is a decision time of monumental importance for our great nation.

As a conclusion to the "work-up" of our patient, we have gathered facts from a thorough history and physical examination, we have examined data from our laboratory of statistics, and we have studied the epidemiologic observations of studious historians. It has been my professional experience that patients and their families will endure study for just so long. The step of inductive diagnosis is the physician's first offering of opinion, and I respectfully suggest that now is the time to proceed with that vital element of case management.

Chapter X

A Tentative Diagnosis

The title of this chapter is not a medical "cop-out." All physicians, whether in research or patient care, are trained to theoretically induce a coherent explanation for any given gathering of data that needs to be understood. Until that theory is tested for efficacy, the theory, in this case diagnosis, is considered tentative. This research model was first described by Francis Bacon (1561–1626), the imaginative British jurist of the sixteenth century.

The explosion of inductive research at the end of the nineteenth century gave rise to the need for medical specialization as advised by Dr. Abraham Flexner in 1910, the creation of the National Research Council by President Woodrow Wilson in 1916, and, eventually, to the research arm of the federal government, the National Institutes of Health, by the U.S. Public Health Service in 1930. Adherence to that model, and today's testing of induced theories in double- and triple-blind multicentric studies, gives definition to honest investigation. This is the accepted and reliable road to all new knowledge.

In chapters 3 and 4, "Faltering Health" and "What Seems to be the Problem?" we discussed the abundance of sociological issues begging to be understood. Before you read any further, I would invite you to induce your own theoretical, tentative diagnosis. What, in your opinion, has been going on in the USA during the last half of the twentieth century and the first decade of the twenty-first?

While you are doing that, I would like to explain that my broader view of health is the consequence of a liberal-arts, premedical education at Ursinus College. Ursinus is a small college near Philadelphia that has always required that each undergraduate student, regardless of major, include a core curriculum that involves the humanities. Consequently, although I was a science, premedical major, my most admired professor was Dr. Charles Mattern, who taught in both the English and philosophy departments. He helped me to think logically and critically.

Philosophy examinations are usually subjective in nature, and to one of his questions in Philosophy 101, I brought my own seventeen-year-old, Doylestown, homespun, Christian-values-oriented answer. I remember no other test paper during my twenty-two years of formal education, but at the top of this one, he wrote, "Young man, you have wisdom beyond your years." As you can see, I treasured his praise and am pleased that today at Ursinus, each freshman is required to participate in a Common Intellectual Experience (CIE). This experience involves assigned diverse readings, small-group discussions among faculty and students with varied majors, and conversations dealing with some of life's most basic questions. What a great way to set the stage for a four-year residential education in preparation for service to humankind.

As described in Carolyn's story, careful listening is often the best tool of the diagnostician. Malaise, that vague sense of ill-being, is commonly the driving force behind the patient's appointment. In the confidential confines of the consultation room, the uninhibited opportunity to express oneself can be most revealing. The inclination to cry out for wholeness just seems to be an innate expression of human nature.

And, as discussed previously in chapter 8, families, cultures, and nations collectively possess the same hopes. In our own nation's history, populist uprisings have periodically given expression to concerns about social imperfection, and our evolution toward a "more perfect union" is still in healthy process.

Can the malaise of our day be seen in the populist "tea parties" of the past two years? Is the citizenry restless about its drift in recent decades toward an entitlement-driven, government-dominated, and debt-burdened political disappointment? Are economic concerns the problem, or are they the symptoms of an underlying malady? Can our collective anxiety be better understood through the historic observations of Arnold Toynbee? Is there a very natural human yearning for a healthy, idealistic republic rooted in spiritual liberty?

Now, let us turn to my tentative diagnosis. After reflection upon all of the data, I am of the considered opinion that our nation is struggling with an identity crisis of growing proportions. "Who am I?" has always been one of life's most basic questions, one each person asks of himself or herself. And collectively, during our first two hundred years, the accepted answer for our nation was that "we are a Christian nation." Our religious roots, Declaration of Independence, Constitution, motto "In God We Trust," and pledge to be "One Nation Under God" all supported that conclusion. Likewise, our works gave credibility and meaning to our beliefs: a bloody civil war to end the evil of slavery, our recognition of the rights of women, a public school system to eradicate ignorance and illiteracy, participation in two world wars abroad to protect all people from oppression, our generous contributions to postwar reconstruction for friend and foe alike, and our provision of a home for the United Nations in the hope that future discord might be solved diplomatically.

From the standpoint of wholeness, the diagnosis of identity crisis is a very serious tentative consideration. At the individual level, self-esteem—an affirmative sense of self-worth—is basic to happiness and accomplishment. We desire it and foster it within our own children by aggressively identifying and cultivating their talents. Loss of self-esteem is always a part of depression and its ultimate tragic form of expression. By describing herself as a terrible person, and by her depressive mood swing, Carolyn was really confessing in my office to a deterioration of self-image, a personal disappointment in self. I now regard the national anxiety, depression, and malaise of the past half century to be the emotional expression of our nation's deteriorating self-image.

There is an amusing story told of the first-grade teacher endeavoring to help her new students realize identity and self-worth. She did this by going down each row asking each student to speak his or her own name.

She came to a little boy who gave his name as "Poe."

"And your first name?"

"Edgar," he responded.

"My goodness, I'll bet your middle name is Allen."

Little boy: "That's right."

"Children, this little boy is named after Edgar Allen Poe, a famous American poet."

The little boy responded, "No ma'am, I *am* Edgar Allen Poe!"

That day the teacher learned a little bit about self-worth.

This chapter is constructed to identify the healthy self-image of the 1950s and to describe the erosion of self-worth that has transpired since that time. Cultivation of healthy self-esteem is at the very heart of Christian teaching. One of the first songs learned in Sunday school is titled "Jesus Loves Me, This I Know." Self-worth is captured in the opening words of the Declaration of Independence. Its preservation is assured by our Bill of

Rights. And the power of it is responsible for personal ambition, creativity, and the happiness of realized fulfillment.

The forces responsible for our declining sense of self-worth and increased sense of vague malaise will be discussed later in more detail. Here, let it only be said that the domestic movement to absolutely separate church and state is being exploited by some to eradicate our identity as a Christian nation.

Francis Collins, in his elegant book *The Language of God,* suggests the simplest explanation for problems is usually the best. Indeed, "the physicist Ernest Rutherford commented more than one hundred years ago that 'a theory that you can't explain to a bartender is probably no damn good.' " In accordance with my invitation to each reader in paragraph three of this chapter, your tentative diagnosis may be different from mine. Indeed, you may have concluded that there is no problem and that our nation's health is not faltering. So be it! These kinds of struggles between doctors are commonplace.

Like all well-trained physicians, my mind is always open to any other rational explanation for the sense of disturbed national wholeness of chapter 3.

In the meantime, let's look at the 1963 struggle of our own Supreme Court, as it provided twentieth-century meaning for the separation clause of our Constitution's First Amendment.

Chapter XI

The Sterilization of Conscience?

Historically based and sociologically sound observations have been made that nations, empires, and cultures fight for identity when they are young, poor, lean, humble, and idealistic. Frequently, when they become old, affluent, "fat," proud, and secular, they fade and collapse. I am not sure that such a process is in progress in our great nation. I do wish, however, that there was some meaningful way to convey to my grandchildren the magnitude of the sacrifices made by my parents and grandparents. But there I go again, lecturing like an old-timer who has personally known six generations.

As I see it from the perspective of time, I cannot help but see a relationship between our declining sense of identity, or self-worth, as it were, and the increasing impact of the debate relating to separation of church and state. As valid as that judgment may have been constitutionally, I strongly suspect that our Supreme Court justices were somewhat apprehensive about the long-term implications and exploitations of that decision in June of 1963. Let me share with you a portion of the opinion of the Court, as delivered by Mr. Justice Clark (Supreme Court Reporter 374 U.S. 212):

United States Supreme Court Building. The pledge of allegiance to our flag ends with the phrase "with liberty and justice for all". To define our nation we often refer to it as a republic governed by "the rule of law". Making law by the legislature and enforcing law by our executive branch of government are important, but our balance of power is dependent in large part upon the judicial interpretation of our common law in the best interest of our common good. Our founding fathers established that system to assure the perpetuation of social order for a citizenry that adored liberty. In today's political environment of multimillion dollar campaign coffers, that citizenry justifiably wonders if the creation, interpretation and enforcement of our law by elected officials is too often the consequence of special interest monetary gifts, rather than the product of patriotic, rational, civic deliberation.

"It is true that religion has been closely identified with our history and government. As we said in Engel v. Vitale, 370 U.S 421, 434, 82 S. Ct. 1261, 1268, 8 L.Ed. 2nd 601 (1962), 'The history of man is inseparable from the history of religion. And since the beginning of that history many people have devoutly believed that more things are wrought by prayer than this world ever dreams of.' In Zorach v. Clauson, 343 U.S. 306, 313, 72 S. Ct. 679, 684, 96 L.Ed. 954 (1952), we gave specific recognition to the proposition that 'we are a religious people whose institutions pre-suppose a Supreme Being.' The fact that the Founding Fathers believed devotedly that there was a God and that the unalienable rights of man were rooted in Him is clearly evidenced in their writings, from the Mayflower Compact to the Constitution itself. This background is evidenced today in our public life through the continuance in our oaths of office from the Presidency to the Alderman of the final supplication, 'So help me God.' Likewise each House of the Congress provides through its Chaplain an opening prayer, and the sessions of this Court are declared open by the crier in a short ceremony, the final phrase of which invokes the grace of God. Again, there are such manifestations in our military forces, where those of our citizens who are under the restrictions of military service wish to engage in voluntary worship. Indeed, only last year an official survey of the country indicated that 64% of our people have church membership, Bureau of the Census, U.S. Department of Commerce, Statistical Abstract of the United States (83d ed. 1962), 48, while less than 3% profess no religion whatever. Id., at p. 46. It can be truly said therefore that today as in the beginning, our national life reflects a religious people who, in the words of Madison, 'are earnestly praying, as in duty bound, that the Supreme Lawgiver of the Universe guide them into every measure which may be worthy of His blessing.' Memorial and Remonstrance Against Religious Assessments, quoted in Everson v. Board of Education, 330 U.S. 1, 71-72, 67 S. Ct. 504, 538-539. 91 L.Ed. 'The government is neutral and while protecting all, it prefers none, and it disparages none.'

"Before examining this 'neutral' position in which the Establishment and Free Exercise Clauses of the First Amendment place our Government, it is well that we discuss the reach of the Amendment under the cases of this Court.

"This Court has decisively settled that the First Amendment's mandate that 'Congress shall make no law respecting an establishment of religion, or prohibiting the free exercise thereof' has been made wholly applicable to the states by the Fourteenth Amendment. Twenty-three years ago in Cantwell v. Connecticut, 310 U.S. 296, 303, 60 S. Ct.

"Our religious composition makes us a vastly more diverse people than were our forefathers. They knew differences chiefly among Protestant sects. Today the Nation is far more heterogeneous religiously, including as it does substantial minorities not only of Catholics and Jews but as well of those who worship according to no version of the Bible and those who worship no God at all. See Torcaso v. Watkins, 367 U.S. 488, 495, 81 S. Ct. 1680, 1683, 6 L.Ed. 2d 982. In the face of such profound changes, practices which may have been objectionable to no one in the time of Jefferson and Madison may today be highly offensive to many persons, the deeply devout and the non-believers alike.

"Whatever Jefferson and Madison would have thought of Bible reading or the recital of the Lord's Prayer in the what few public schools existed in their day, our use of the history of their time must limit itself to broad purposes, not specific practices. By such a standard, I am persuaded, as is the Court, that the devotional exercises carried on in the Baltimore and Abington schools offend the First Amendment because they sufficiently threaten in our day those substantive evils the fear of which call for the Establishment Clause of the First Amendment. It is 'a constitution we are expounding' and our interpretation of the First Amendment must necessarily be responsive to the much more highly charged nature of religious questions in contemporary society.

"The American experiment in free public education available to all children has been guided in large measure by the dramatic evolution of the religious diversity among the population which our public schools serve."

In light of this eloquent exposition on the First Amendment and its application to our increasingly diverse citizenry, we must ask the question, "Is it possible to have our cake and eat it, too?" That is, is it possible to separate church and state in an absolute sense and still maintain an ethic that is conducive to societal wholeness? Is it possible to respect diversity and yet accomplish harmonious unity? Or, is it possible to live longer and still enjoy it more? I would respectfully suggest that the answer to each of these questions is yes.

Once again, the USA is labeled a Christian nation by virtue of historic and statistical fact. The healthy separation of church and state need not mean a sterilization of conscience. To the contrary, as an act of religious and national patriotism, the Christian church in the USA and the churches, synagogues, and temples of other faiths have a twenty-first-century opportunity to proclaim the unique ideas that have made this a great nation.

Aside from consideration of religions and denominations, it should be apparent to even the most casual observers of history that members of our strange species are capable of great cruelty and great compassion. Is human nature best characterized by the Adolf Hitlers, Joseph Stalins, and Ted Bundys; or do the Mother Teresas, Albert Schweitzers, and Irena Sendlers more accurately represent our inclinations? Let us direct our attention to goodness and badness.

Chapter XII

Grace, Gratitude, and Greatness

During our first two hundred years, most agree that the USA has evolved to the status of greatness. The implications of my discussion suggest that "greatness" is in some way related to or even synonymous with "goodness." What, pray tell, is "goodness"?

As usual, I am interested in Noah Webster's opinion. Because of the elusive nature of that quality, Webster begins by identifying "goodness" as "the state of being good." No help there! For purposes of clarification, he goes on with an alternative explanation: "the nutritious, flavorful, or beneficial part of something." As a guy who loves to garden and eat, I can relate to that.

The adjective "great," of course, describes the noun "nation." The nation USA is the sociological object of our concern. Consequently, the farmer in me wants to know, in a worldcentric sense, is our nation a nutritious, flavorful, and beneficial part of the international community? Or, flawed as we have always been, is our evolving domestic and international goodness in the process of slowdown?

For me the understanding of goodness began with my parents, who seemed always involved in helping some less-fortunate person. The understanding of the relationship between that helpfulness and reverence was cultivated by the Doylestown Presbyterian and Baptist churches, the Boy Scouts of America, a brief Bible reading and meditation to start each public grade-school day, and even compulsory 10 a.m. weekday chapel services at my undergraduate Evangelical and Reformed college, named for Zacharias Ursinus of the sixteenth century.

As a growing child, being good and doing good did not come naturally. As a young pianist, I did not enjoy our family pilgrimages to Almshouse Road on glorious Sunday afternoons to play hymns for the old folks living in what was then called the Bucks County Poorhouse. Sunday evening lawn-chair hymn sings on the banks of the Neshaminy Creek at the Neshaminy-Warwick Presbyterian Church seemed especially boring. As we would sing "Day is Dying in the West," the competing desire to wade out into that lovely stream with hip boots, creel, and fly rod to match wits with one of God's pound-for-pound most-combative creatures was ever present. As a tight end with pretty good hands, I considered the community Thanksgiving morning worship services to be distracting. After all, as a three-year letterman with all-conference Bucks Mont credentials, I had to be ready to catch important passes after lunch at the annual Doylestown-Lansdale Turkey Day football game.

Today those resented "training camp" experiences are among my most treasured memories. The pursuit of "Service Above Self," the motto of Rotary Clubs, still involves personal discipline, but the human complexity of motivation, personal reward, and reciprocal meaning have become issues of curious intrigue.

Between 1946 and 1948, in the early years of Clyde's illness, I interrupted my premedical education to serve in Korea with the United States Army. World War II had just ended and had been considered to be a just war. Military service on behalf of "goodness" was still admired by all, and the GI Bill benefits provided the economic assurance for medical school expenses. Behind all of this careful planning, and mentioned to no one, was the hope that Anne and I could marry while she taught in the public schools and I attended graduate school. That all happened as planned, but, unknown to me at that time, forces behind the scenes were shaping my own opportunities for goodness to humankind.

In a major scientific breakthrough, the electron microscope had been developed in 1935, and viruses were seen for the first time. As tissue-specific organisms, the use of tissue cultures soon gave rise to the cultivation of these organisms, modifications of their disease potential, and the development of vaccines for all viral diseases. Although smallpox prevention, using the cowpox virus since 1799, had set the example, it was not until 1955 that Jonas Salk announced the availability of an injectable polio vaccine—ten years too late for Clyde.

A few years later, Albert Sabin improved on the idea with a live polio vaccine that could be given by mouth. This new vaccine would provide intestinal and blood antibody protection for the person, but, if given to population masses, would spread to almost everyone, providing "herd immunity," a complete eradication of a home for the wild virus that caused death and paralysis. We were in the early years of Clyde's sad story when, in 1963, I was invited by organized medicine in general, and the Chester County Medical Society in particular, to develop a program that would "herd immunize" the 250,000 citizens of Chester County. With much assistance from doctors, nurses, our public school system, and many volunteers, we administered the vaccine drops on sugar cubes on three SOS days (Sabin Oral Sundays). Long lines of people received one dose of each of the three strains of vaccine, and, as a matter of insistence by county residents, each contributed twenty-five cents per dose. The money more than paid expenses, and the $50,000 residuum created a public health foundation that continues to benefit the public health needs of the county. Not a single case of indigenous polio has been detected in Chester County since that time. Voluntarism, that great feature of our Christian nation, continues to accomplish much good outside the tax structure of big government.

The administration of this vaccine continued around the globe until the early 1970s, when the World Health Organization reported that the disease was almost completely eradicated in the developed nations, but was still epidemic in the third-world, developing nations. For this reason, in 1972 the World Health Organization developed an Expanded Program on Immunization (EPI), but, because of insufficient infrastructure, it had reached less than 5 percent of third-world children by 1985.

Between 1980 and 1985, the vaccine had been used in one developing, tropical country with great success. This program had been implemented by the Rotarians of the Philippine Islands, who were able to provide the transportation and refrigeration needed to reach remote villages. Using this as a model, Dr. Carlos Conseco, a Mexican pediatrician serving as the president of Rotary International in 1984–1985, conferred with his friend, Dr. Albert Sabin, about the possibility of using that plan to accomplish worldwide "herd" immunization and disease eradication. The only other infectious disease to have been eradicated in the world's history was small-pox in 1979—an almost two-hundred-year effort.

Between them, Drs. Sabin and Conseco had developed a tentative time-table to raise the funds needed for vaccine purchase between 1986 and 1988, to administer the vaccine for disease control between 1989 and 1995, and to focus on cleanup and disease eradication between 1996 and the year 2000. Having been a Rotary district governor in 1980, I was asked to help raise the money in Phase I—another anti-polio volunteer invitation!

With one hundred million third-world births each year, at a vaccine cost of twelve cents per child, the ten-year immunization program was very roughly estimated to be a $120 million vaccine cost effort. I was sent with many others to Rotary International headquarters in Evanston, Illinois, to be trained as a fundraiser and was assigned the four Rotary districts in eastern Pennsylvania and two in north and south New Jersey.

Rotary clubs were in existence in over 170 countries, and the basic plan was to raise most of the money in the developed nations and to use Rotarians in third-world nations to organize mass vaccine administration projects. My six districts raised an average of $1 million each, and at the Rotary International Convention in Philadelphia in 1988, it was announced that in contrast to the $120 million need, $250 million had been pledged worldwide.

Third-world National Immunization Days were implemented as planned, and by the year 2000, the annual global number of cases of polio had fallen from five hundred thousand to fewer than five thousand. The World Health Organization, the Pan American Health Organization (PAHO), the U.S. Centers for Disease Control and Prevention (CDC), many national governments, and many other volunteers had joined in this collaborative effort. Unfortunately, civil strife and transportation problems have interfered with the access to all children in third-world countries, and although the eradication goal of the year 2000 was not realized, the number of reported cases is now fewer than one thousand per year in just five nations. The program is still in operation.

There has been no polio in the Western Hemisphere for more than a decade, and, as a result of its efforts, Rotary International has received the highest recognition from the CDC, PAHO, and the World Health Organization and has been selected as a Non-Governmental Organization (NGO) in the United Nations (UN).

This sculpted memorial by Glenna Goodacre depicts humankind's hope for the eradication of poliomyelitis. It stands in front of the headquarters of Rotary International in Evanston, IL. The project to accomplish that, launched by Rotary in 1988, has had a dramatic impact on the disease and is still in process. Those of us involved in the initiation of the effort were motivated by the plea, "the children are waiting". Unfortunately, due to civil unrest and ill-conceived issues of resistance, some of the children in developing nations are still waiting. The determined and costly finalization of complete eradication is now being supported by generous matching gifts from the foundation established by Bill and Melinda Gates.

I have focused your attention in this chapter on some of my family's voluntary goodness in an effort to recognize the fact that a healthy nation's ethic has a dynamic dimension. The voluntary willingness to help the less fortunate is an integral part of almost every belief system. Indeed, to do unto others as we would have them do unto us is "the golden rule" with widespread acceptance. In a Christian sense, that voluntary goodness is the grateful response to God's amazing grace. By feeding the hungry, clothing the naked, visiting the sick and imprisoned, and helping the poor, we are expressing our gratitude for all that He has done for us. For centuries, faith-based humanitarian voluntarism from within the masses has accomplished much to alleviate human suffering.

Chapter XIII

The Dependency of Independence on Dependence

As a relatively young nation, the United States of America is still looked upon by many as an experimental "test tube." Located on an isolated continent, it is surrounded by water except for two basically friendly borders. It is rich with mountains, valleys, inland rivers, plains, and a latitudinal location conducive to productivity. We pledge allegiance to a flag "and to the republic for which it stands," and our first two centuries of productivity and happiness are inclined to suggest experimental success. However, I have been discussing evolving flaws and, justifiably, am endeavoring to understand their meaning.

The Declaration of Independence that gave identity to our new nation in 1776 declared the self-evident truth that a Creator regarded each person to be of equal value and bestowed on each certain unalienable human rights. These ideas had been discussed philosophically in Europe for many years, but this document was designed to actually bring about a kind of government that would put those beliefs into action. A republic, wherein the power was to reside in its people, was unnatural, and this Declaration, the Constitution, and the Bill of Rights would have been considered liberal or radical in their day.

In the previous chapter I discussed the voluntary goodness that was evident during the first half of the twentieth century. For most Americans that goodness was a natural expression of gratitude for our gracious Creator's generosity. Those generations appreciated freedom, endured insecurity, applied their own industry and creativity, and lived to enjoy comfort, happiness, and patriotic pride. I comment on those milestones to again call your attention to the civilization cycle. My loving parents and grandparents participated in the creation of that legacy. As a result of many sacrifices made by them, I think that we can safely say that we have now moved into an age of affluence.

Income levels have increased, the stock market has soared, real estate values have grown, and life expectancy has almost doubled. In spite of this, we have reported a long list of sociological and emotional misfortunes that have transpired during the past sixty years. Is it possible that our grand experiment is still in process and that these recent years of behavioral confusion are but the adolescence of a young nation? Having discussed goodness at some length, let me make a few observations relating to that great mystery of human nature, "badness."

In my younger years I often wondered why that rabbinical allegory in Genesis did not depict Adam's misbehavior as having beaten, murdered, or sexually violated Eve; or why the two of them didn't tear up or burn down the garden. All they did was eat an apple! Last week the young woman who cleans our home was commenting on my summer vegetables. I explained to her that my interest in horticulture was a hand-me-down from my father, who loved his vegetable garden. In a moment of jest I told her that my father used to say, "If Adam and Eve had behaved themselves, we wouldn't have all these darn weeds!" "Yes", she replied, "we must all learn to trust and obey." From the mouths of babes...!

As I recall, the apple had something to do with disobedience, the acquisition of knowledge and wisdom, and a rejection of the need for a Creator. Is it possible that by virtue of our overpowering affluence, our technologic advances, and our management of life expectancy itself, we know all things and have become our own gods? Is it possible that we have forgotten that our independence was dependent in its moment of conception on the self-evident truths of a Creator? The prodigal temptation to believe in our own self-sufficiency is universal, and that is bad news for the fragile concept of republic—an ideal that requires the constant nourishment of goodness.

J. B. Phillips warns us, in his fine book *Your God is Too Small*, that rational wrestling matches in the world of theology are risky at best. Omnipotence and eternity are concepts quite beyond human comprehension. As a physician who lives with his own medical theology, however, I can only say that God is at least as large as my own comprehension. Within that limitation, my own rational wrestling match is still in process.

Irena Sendler, savior of children in the Warsaw ghetto, died on May 12, 2008, at the age of ninety-eight. As a doctor's daughter, she had been brought up in a home that was open to anyone in pain or need, Jew or Gentile. She was born to selflessness and rejected anti-Jewish discrimination in prewar Poland, during Nazi occupation, and during postwar Soviet-imposed Communist rule. The penalty for helping Jews was instant execution, but she organized a rescue scheme that smuggled a large number of Jewish children out of the Nazi Warsaw ghetto of four hundred thousand souls. In 1983, a tree was planted in her honor at Yad Vashem Jerusalem, and in 2003 she received Poland's highest honor, the Order of the White Eagle. Irena claimed that no religion motivated her: she acted from "the need of my heart." Without identifying a specific religion, such goodness may be religion in its purest form. I am sure that history is punctuated by such examples of individual humanitarianism, but they are the exception. In my own experience, goodness and badness are in constant conflict, and too often the love of money, power, and security lead to the selection of the low road.

This chapter on our nation's recent rational wrestling match is again a reflection on human nature. I have heard the subject discussed in a variety of settings, and whether it's referred to as goodness and badness, humility and pride, selflessness and selfishness, generosity and greed, maturity and immaturity, beneficial and destructive social behavior, good and evil, or righteousness and sin, we are all talking about the same thing. The struggle within each person is just a fact. The correspondence of Mother Teresa recently discussed in *Newsweek* magazine shed an interesting light on her own struggle.

Rotary and its wonderful foundation are fine organizations and accomplish much good, but, like most organizations trying to motivate generosity and good works, they have recognition plaques for your walls, badges for your chest, pins for your lapels, and medallions for your neck. Having been a district governor, I was asked recently to conduct a formal induction of my club's new president. I introduced my responsibility by acquainting my audience with my early evening preparation:

Little Bob Poole

Sat down on a stool

To pull on his socks and black tie,

He reached for his jewelry,

Put on that tomfoolery,

And said, "What a good boy am I."

No disrespect for Rotary, but a commentary on the strange species into which we have been born—*Homo sapiens*—a species within which humility and pride, laughter and tears, and goodness and badness are never far apart.

My little parody, of course, was a takeoff on:

Little Jack Horner

Sat in a corner

Eating his Christmas pie

He stuck in his thumb

And pulled out a plum

And said, "What a good boy am I."

As a child, I could never understand Jack's justification. What is so good about pulling a plum out of a pie? I know very little about Mother Goose theology, but it has been suggested that the pie was an undeserved Christmas gift from a loving father and in it he discovered the plum of amazing grace.

The separation of church and state was a brilliant decision by our Constitution's framers. The true church cannot objectively evaluate our nation's behavior if it is part of the political mix. But, as members of that church, each citizen must be aware of the nation's dependence of independence on healthy beliefs. The subtle drift into greed, apathy, weakness, vulnerability, and ultimate bondage is the known risk of civilized history's cycle. We are in a position to halt that drift and to return to the values of our nation's youth.

Our ultimate goal is a remedy. And whether our faltering health is a manifestation of adolescent indecision or adult rebellion, the "patient USA" justifiably asks, "Doctor, what do you recommend to help me again regain a state of wellness?"

Section Four

Therapeutic Management

Chapter XIV

Therapeutics 101

Believe it or not, we are now prepared to discuss a treatment program for the "patient USA." Like all well-trained physicians, we have taken a careful history, we have physically examined the whole person, and we have reviewed some supporting laboratory data. From these facts, hopefully, we have induced a tentative diagnosis: a gradually evolving loss of identity.

In the world of health care, the restoration of wholeness means implementing the therapeutic measures to effect cure, or to eradicate illness, or to regain one's health, or to just "get better." And it is a marvelous thing to behold! I am now four weeks post-op, have rejoined the human race, and will be able to get rid of the walker and drive my own car in the near future. But pain and disability, dependency on others, and inconvenience are still sufficiently fresh in my mind that a sincere sense of gratitude for what can be done is ever present.

As I endeavor to draw a parallel between my own experience and the subject of this book, *My Uncle Sam Needs a House Call*, I am reminded of the basics required for just "getting better." First, one must recognize and admit that a problem exists; next comes the establishment of an accurate causative diagnosis; and last, one must pursue a definitive cure. Those basics are required of this great nation under study. By now I hope that we are all in agreement that health, in its fullest sense, involves our physical bodies, our emotional reactions, our sociological relationships, and our belief systems. I am also hopeful that most readers can identify with the distressing, national, sociological events of the past sixty years to agree with the general impression of "faltering health."

When confronted with illness, the ultimate interest of the medical community centers on a remedy that works. Not infrequently, why it works and how it works is only understood with the passage of time. In 1928 a Scottish physician and bacteriologist by the name of Alexander Fleming noted that cultured bacterial colonies on a petri dish were suppressed if they were located near contaminant mold colonies of *Penicillium notatum*. Not until 1938 did Oxford scientists Florey and Chain discover why this was so. The mold colonies were manufacturing and emitting a chemical substance that they called penicillin. The therapeutic efficacy of this curative discovery was exercised for many years before the "how" was understood—that is, the enzymatic interference within bacterial metabolism.

My professor of therapeutics at the Jefferson Medical College in 1951 was Dr. Martin E. Rehfuss. Dr. Rehfuss was one of the last "old school" faculty members, serving Jefferson as a professor of clinical medicine from 1914 to 1956. He was a physically handsome man with a distinguished profile, a curled, waxed mustache, and an always-impeccable attire that included his signature white vest and sparkling gold chain. His introductory lecture in pharmacology began, "Gentlemen (the Jefferson student body was all male at that time), the therapeutic management of illness must be both symptomatic and definitive."

His point, of course, was that some remedies such as aspirin and good old belladonna are designed to provide patient comfort. Other drugs, such as penicillin, are definitive in nature and effect a cure by actually combating the cause. He stressed the importance and simultaneous use of both and assured his young students that the physician who neglected patient comfort would never develop a substantial practice. Similarly, we must always be attentive to underlying cause if our therapeutic plan is to accomplish definitive cure.

With this therapeutic model in mind, let us construct a treatment plan that will alleviate that troublesome symptom of malaise and also be sure to find a definitive measure that will restore the "patient USA" again to a state of wholeness and greatness.

The well-worn cliché of "no pain, no gain" is commonly applicable to "getting better," and our recovery as a nation will certainly involve sacrifice. It seems to me that the situation suggests there are three major symptoms contributing to our national sense of ill-being. To accomplish patient comfort, attention should be directed to:

1. The symptomatic alleviation of embarrassment. I am convinced that our nation is justifiably ashamed of our divorce rates, crime rates, educational failings, and lingering social injustice. We need a renewed realization of patriotic pride.

2. The symptomatic alleviation of adversarialism. We need to regain a sense of trust within our own human family and a restoration of neighborliness.

3. The symptomatic alleviation of an insidious sense of creeping servitude. Have we successfully preserved the republic so carefully crafted by our founding fathers? Are we served by or have we become servants of our federal government?

Concerned citizens ask, "What can I do? How can I help?" Symptomatic therapy is the area where good works are needed. Problems deserve study, and effective solutions need implementation. Motivated by a common devotion to national goodness and greatness, the alleviation of symptoms can restore the sense of well-being that characterizes wholeness.

As you read these next three chapters on the management of symptoms, may I respectfully request your patience with the author. The story is told of the stuttering little old lady bridge player who took almost six minutes to stammer out the suggestion that "this would be a better world if we would just stop all the wars, send all troops home, and mandate the disarmament of all nations." Her partners, anxious to keep the game going, replied, "Gertrude, that's easy for you to say!"

Our discussion of symptoms will refer to some of the stickiest problems of our day—and they do deserve rational confrontation. Let me only say now that resolution of these enigmas can most easily be accomplished in the loving environment that will be discussed in chapter 18, "Definitive Therapy."

Chapter XV

The Relief of Embarrassment

Before we begin our most important discussion of therapy, let me comment on the precarious subject of labels. I am sure that the readers of my first thirteen chapters have concluded that this author is hopelessly conservative. I would suppose that this conclusion is justified in the context of twenty-first century understanding. On the other hand, my reading of history suggests that the ideas that I hold dear, the ideas that have evolved into a great nation that commands the admiration of humankind worldwide—these are the liberal ideas of 1776. To suggest that a citizenry could be sovereign, that its government should be relatively small and servile, and that a nation would voluntarily look out for its own, violates the experience of recorded world history. Truly, the experiment is still in process, and what we are is still considered to be sociologically radical. So much for labels!

And again, so much has happened since I first picked up my pen thirteen months ago that a comment on current events should precede any discussion of treatment. From the standpoint of Toynbee's civilization cycle, it would appear that we have, during my lifetime, moved from the stage of "comfort, happiness, and pride" into the stage of "affluence." The greatest threat of affluence is to be seen in the next stages of "greed and apathy," considered by some to be the inevitable, determined movement of all cultures and civilizations. Symptoms of greed are already to be seen in the pursuit of outrageous wealth by our captains of industry, the reckless spending of those with a multiplicity of credit cards, the exploitation of the get-rich-quick hopefuls by Ponzi promises and lottery improbabilities, a federal government that has incurred national indebtedness in excess of $13 trillion, and speculative investment portfolios that reflect high-risk expectations. I have been told by informed economists that the Dow Jones Industrial Average of October 2007 that exceeded 14,000 was more likely an unrealistic bubble created by smoke and mirrors. One of those experts considered the economic events of 2008 a correction, not a recession.

Our second significant current event of note relates to an electorate that is overwhelmingly white electing a handsome family of color to the position of national leadership. As a family physician with concerns for my nation and its frail families, I am encouraged to see that our new president is a devout family man; that beyond the burdens of his office, he loves his wife, adores his daughters, and vows to budget family time as a responsibility of high priority. As an old basketball player, I can also relate to his love for that commitment of time. I strongly suspect that the world is as astonished as we are by our democratic recognition of this family's merit.

With those current events in place, let us direct our attention to the relief of our patient's malaise, that vague sense of ill-being that is so discomforting to so many of our citizens. We are motivated by a wholesome sense of patriotism, accustomed to a reputation for excellence, but a bit embarrassed by the evidences of greed described above, the widening gulf between the rich and the poor, the evolution of many center-city ghettoes, our soaring crime and incarceration rates, the progressive instability of the nuclear family, a struggling health care system, immoral behavior among elected and church officials, the abuse of children, violation of women, and the deterioration of our public school system. As a nation we are justifiably concerned that among thirty industrialized nations, our students rank twenty-fifth in math and twenty-first in college graduation rates—we were first twenty-five years ago. Some call this component of malaise guilt. Some call it concern or shame. Because of its relationship to our collective conscience, I have elected to more gently label it as embarrassment—and we should be ashamed!

Recently, the Senate of the State of Kansas called on its chaplain, the Reverend Joe Wright of the Central Christian Church, for an invocation to open legislative deliberations. His words received national attention, and Joe has been described as "a pastor with guts." I was recently asked to deliver an invocation for our regular weekly Rotary Club meeting and modified Joe's courageous remarks, as follows:

"Dear Lord and Father of us all:

As Rotarians struggling to do good, we pause and ask for your forgiveness for the nation that gave birth to the service club movement of 1905.

We pollute the air with profanity and call it "freedom of expression."

We have neglected to discipline our children and call it "building self-esteem,"

We have exploited the poor and call it "the lottery,"

We have coveted our neighbor's possessions and call it "ambition,"

We decry rape and child abuse but foster readily available pornography and call it "art,"

We have abused power and call it "politics,"

We give lip service to our belief in the sanctity of life but terminate the lives of thousands of unborn children each day and call it "choice."

We invest countless hours in the vain, the vulgar, and the vacuous and call it "entertainment."

We have greedily surrounded ourselves with costly comforts, paid for them with borrowed money, sent the bill to our grandchildren. and call it "deficit spending."

In effect, we have neglected the values of our forefathers and call it "enlightenment."

As Rotarians, we ask for your blessing upon this food, and with the Psalmist, we individually pray, "Create in me a clean heart, O God: and renew a right spirit within me."

Is it possible that as a nation we are rationalizing an erudite, progressive misinterpretation to our constitutional documents in an effort to justify our sadly regressive interpersonal behavior?

But again, the reader asks, "What can I do, how can I help?" President John F. Kennedy was hopeful that each of us would "ask not what your country can do for you; ask what you can do for your country." Let me begin my discussion of symptomatic relief by making a positive observation. This embarrassment, or shame, is felt by large numbers of patriotic traditionalists, suggesting that a collective conscience is still alive. Shame, in actuality, is a lingering expression of our nation's sense of goodness. As with Carolyn, our sensitivity to our shortcomings is a good place to begin in our quest to regain patriotic pride or healthy self-esteem.

May I respectfully suggest that many of these issues of embarrassment have in common the legalization of self-indulgence as an entitlement, an event that has gradually evolved during the past half century. Our Bill of Rights was added to our Constitution as the first ten amendments to assure the preservation of personal liberty. Two hundred years later, we rationalize that these amendments imply the constitutional rights of each citizen to do as he or she pleases—that self-indulgence supersedes self-discipline as a right. Arnold Toynbee, in his *Study of History*, points out in his chapters on "The Breakdowns and Disintegration of Civilizations" that hedonism and greed are common forces at work in this part of the cycle. People turn away from belief systems of hard times, a process he calls "spiritual demoralization"; social leaders abandon creativity and turn to the accumulation of wealth as an end in itself; and, in its affluence, the cultural unit becomes preoccupied with the ecstatic pleasures of drugs and sex. But Toynbee assures his readers that as agents of free will, we can voluntarily inflict social breakdown or unified, progressive achievement upon ourselves at any moment in the cycle.

Alexander Solzhenitsyn, the Nobel Prize-winning Russian author who died on August 3, 2008, at the age of eighty-nine, was a guest speaker at Harvard in 1978. Although he had endured many years of gulag imprisonment by Joseph Stalin for his criticism of communism and socialism, he could already see a decline in the United States of America, characterized by "materialism, the decadence of irresponsible freedom, and the blindness of superiority."

The legacy of liberty intended by our nation's founders relates to the freedom of each citizen to realize personal potential and to live responsibly in the best interest of the group. To further understand that meaning of liberty and the collective conscience of our nation, we need to return to those first eight million immigrants who settled on the eastern shore of our continent and examine the Bibles they carried. We need to review the Judeo-Christian concepts of right and wrong recorded there, Christ's interpretation of them, and the relationship between that scripture and our treasured liberty.

That relationship will be treated more fully in chapter 17 when we discuss definitive therapy. Here let it only be said that the profound impact of Christ's life and teachings on the world and our nation is now a matter of record. Historian Philip Schaff has noted, "This Jesus of Nazareth, without money or arms, conquered more millions of persons than Alexander, Caesar, Mohammed, or Napoleon. Without science or learning, he shed more light on things human and divine than all of the philosophers and scholars combined. Without the eloquence of schools he spoke such words of life as were never spoken before or since, and produced effects that lie beyond the reach of orator or poet. Without writing a single line, he put more pens in motion and furnished themes for more sermons, orations, discussions, learned volumes, works of art, and songs of praise than the whole army of great men and women of ancient and modern times."

I rehearse these matters to remind each reader and myself that it is just a historic fact that during this religion's interface with government, the United States of America became a great nation. Common beliefs gave rise to common mores, which in turn gave rise to common law that was intended for enforcement in the best interest of the common good. And loving God, self, and neighbor was identified as the proactive legal key to all other legalisms. Further, "neighbor" was defined as anyone in need or anyone who provides help.

It was to that ethic that the invitation has been extended to all who seek liberty. The response to that invitation has been one of diversity, a fact that reflects on the commonality of human nature. Indeed, we continue to be a "sweet land of liberty" where equality in our Creator's eyes is respected and endowed human rights are assured.

Treatment of symptoms is, by its very nature, an intellectual exercise. It basically consists of applying the knowledge and wisdom of the day to the problem in question. It is for this reason that think-tanks are composed of experts in a variety of disciplines who, hopefully, will provide insights objectively. At the opening of this chapter we listed a huge variety of embarrassing issues that need that kind of study. Such a study group must be powerfully motivated by a patriotic desire to achieve a solution that will heal and restore the republic. Vested interests, of course, are a normal part of human nature, but the sensitivity of group thinking usually detects self-interest and weighs its value accordingly. Unfortunately, in societies where affluence and greed have gotten out of hand, governmental regulation becomes the expected solution. It should be hoped that such regulation that infringes on the liberty of the citizens would be temporary until definitive therapy restores national health.

As an example of the management of symptoms, let us look at our health care system, which has been deemed broken. Since the beginning of recorded history, people have yearned to live long and well. As mentioned earlier, great scientific strides have been made that have dramatically prolonged life expectancy. As observed by Senator Tom Daschle in his book *What We Can Do About the Health Care Crisis,* "We have some of the world's best specialists and a training system that attracts people from all over the world. We are recognized as world leaders in technological innovation and ground-breaking research. And people with good insurance coverage can choose from a wide range of providers." But the issues of health care involve quality, access, and cost. Health care delivery is a very complex matter, and the issues of access and cost are crying for study and correction by a nation already burdened by heavy debt.

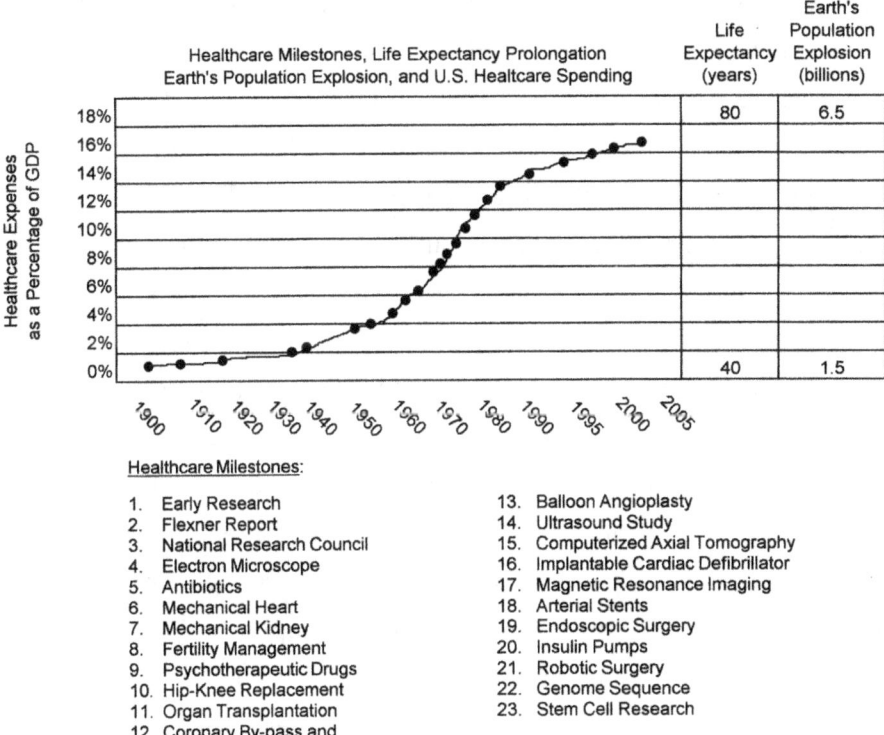

Healthcare Milestones, Life Expectancy Prolongation Earth's Population Explosion, and U.S. Healtcare Spending

Healthcare Milestones:

1. Early Research
2. Flexner Report
3. National Research Council
4. Electron Microscope
5. Antibiotics
6. Mechanical Heart
7. Mechanical Kidney
8. Fertility Management
9. Psychotherapeutic Drugs
10. Hip-Knee Replacement
11. Organ Transplantation
12. Coronary By-pass and

13. Balloon Angioplasty
14. Ultrasound Study
15. Computerized Axial Tomography
16. Implantable Cardiac Defibrillator
17. Magnetic Resonance Imaging
18. Arterial Stents
19. Endoscopic Surgery
20. Insulin Pumps
21. Robotic Surgery
22. Genome Sequence
23. Stem Cell Research

In recent decades much concern has been expressed about the gradual increase in health spending to almost 17% of the Gross Domestic Product. Driven by the human desire to live long and well, clinical research and innovation during the 20th Century has doubled life expectancy, and, in part, has been a contributing factor involved in this economic observation. Many other factors relating to our insatiable thirst for longevity and the need for tort reform factor into the high cost of success.

This powerful value to live long and well has prompted our species to invest heavily in health care. That fact has attracted a multitude of parties with a greed-driven desire to share in that wealth. That throng has collectively contributed to the rising costs that outstrip the growth of the gross domestic product and adversely affect affordability and access. During my practicing years, I lived through the medical economic stages of fee for service, nonprofit insurance, for-profit insurance, government-provided, managed health care delivered, and, now, the for-profit hospital approach to health care delivery. That relentless process produced a counterproductive increase in cost and consequent compromised access. In his book, Senator Daschle offers some interesting problem-solving ideas that consider our national debt. Those ideas need think-tank attention by a group of patriotic physicians, community hospital administrators, economists, lawyers, sociologists, employers, insurance experts, elected officials, and average citizens. Vested interests will constantly threaten such a discussion, but each panel member, as a potential patient and patriotic citizen, has expertise of value to the group.

And what about the deterioration of the public school system? Mandated, disciplined learning was once the essence of its nature, and our national literacy rates and powerful middle class, a product of it. Today, I am told that student bodies that "know their rights," weakened families that have become apathetic, violent behavior that engenders fear, and intimidated faculties that have ceased to fight the system are contributing to an exodus of hopelessness. No issue better exemplifies my call for study and action. Few problems contribute as mightily to our faltering health. My personal love affair with the public school system of the United States of America began in the 1930s, and dedicated teachers, loving discipline, parental support, and the joys of enlightenment are all part of that fond memory.

As a third example of an embarrassing issue, I submit for your consideration the problems of the nuclear family. Strong, healthy cultures depend on the strength and health of these social family units. As a family physician, I have referred with admiration to our forty-fourth president as a devout family man. This second adjective, "family," denotes a priceless value for a society in desperate need of a visible role model.

My wife and I attend our Presbyterian church regularly and look forward this year to the celebration of our sixtieth wedding anniversary. Each Sunday we transport good friends who are in their midnineties and can no longer drive. Those dear folks will celebrate their seventieth anniversary next month. The four of us go dressed in our Sunday best, as was the custom of our generation; we are motivated to worship regularly by gratitude, not fear, and we depart from that experience with a sense of fulfillment and happiness. I mention this meaningful practice because I have become a curious student of serendipity.

Last Sunday a young family sat immediately in front of us. From left to right the family consisted of a clean-cut young father, a youngest son (about three), the oldest son (about eight), an only daughter (about five), and, on the right, an attractive young mother. The dress of the group was clean, tidy, and informal—there is something refreshing about informality that depicts reverence as a seven-day-a-week experience. Little brother seemed to need Dad's arm around his shoulders, but it didn't stifle the kind of stuff that goes on between brothers. The only daughter kept her arm around Mother's waist, while Mom helped her with the reading involved in the programmed service. When it came time for the children's sermon, big brother was the first to bravely march forward with his hands in his pockets. Middle sister was the next to follow but looked back when little brother exhibited reluctance to leave Dad's side. Big sister without hesitation became little Mother, turned back, and took little brother by the hand to provide the needed sense of security. Strong Dad and strong Mom smiled at each other, slid close, and leaned together affectionately during the children's story sermon and prayer.

I must confess that I don't remember much about the content of that service—the old doctor was endeavoring to put this chapter together, and the sermon of the day was sitting right before his eyes. I was looking at the functional dynamics of a healthy nuclear family taking place in a setting conducive to the cultivation of a healthy belief system upon which emotional and social stability are so dependent. Until a better explanation comes along, I shall always regard such simple experiences as serendipitous.

I sincerely hope that those strong parents will see to it that the family sits down together with regularity at the traditional dinner table, where manners are taught, the day's events are discussed, wisdom is imparted, and moral dilemmas are given consideration. Let it only here be said that marriage and family are best defined by simple observations such as this. The healthy, traditional, nuclear family is the psychological and sociological training ground for the discovery of identity, the realization of self-worth, the cultivation of a healthy personal belief system, and the consequential respect for others and joys of fulfillment. Strong nations are dependent on the propagation of strong people by their strong families.

As we all know, there are many forces tearing at the family stability of years gone by. Inflationary economic forces often demand that both parents work. A myriad of attractive activities pull family members in a variety of directions. Television's commercial lure to "have it now and pay for it later" begins with the preschoolers. The corporate world has little respect for the nuclear family and scatters the family mercilessly. These are the unavoidable facts of our day and too often create dysfunctional families comprised of individuals that communicate poorly and pass each other silently like ships in the night.

Add to this scene the impact of the entertainment industry. Newspaper columnist Cal Thomas refers to the world of cable TV as "vain, vulgar, and vacuous." With sex-related crime at an all-time high, should we be concerned that the adult entertainment industry rakes in $3 billion to $13 billion each year; that the pornography industry, on January 8, 2009, asked Congress for a $5 billion bailout to "help rejuvenate the sexual appetite of America"? That audacious appeal is the consequence of the legal rights granted that industry by our twentieth-century understanding of civil liberty.

The importance of strong families to the integrity of society has been given much study. Lawrence G. Brandon, in his book titled *Pathway to Progress*, refers to recent studies that offer overwhelming evidence for the catastrophic effect of fragmented family life on children.

"Since 1970, one million American children a year have seen their parents divorce. One in four children lives with a single parent today, a total of 19,220,000 in the year 2000. Research shows that many, if not most of them, are left emotionally crippled. Too many children of divorce grow into adults who find love and commitment elusive, who move from one unsuitable, unstable relationship to another and, often, replicate their parents' behavior with their own partners and children.

"Research statistics belie the fact that many, many single parents do an absolutely outstanding job in raising their children and protecting them, to the extent possible, from the negative consequences of divorce. Single parents, like married parents, are still parents with a huge important job on their hands—developing young minds and bodies and spirits to be the next generation of adults to make positive contributions to life, love, and work in our society. It can and is being done effectively by millions of parents – be they married or single. The fact remains that it is a much more difficult job if one has to do it alone.

"Both *The Case for Marriage* and *The Unexpected Legacy of Divorce* state that marriage is a vital protector for adults of both sexes and for children, and that its benefits are not replicable in other family structures. For men and women, marriage is actually the best guarantee of health and happiness. Mortality rates are 50 percent higher among unmarried women than for their married counterparts and 250 percent higher among unmarried men. Married people of both sexes have better health, less depression, and fewer other mental disorders than unmarried people. These benefits, according to research conducted by Waite and Gallagher, are not shared by cohabitating couples, who are less sexually faithful, less willing to support each other, and more likely to split up.

Anne and I were married on a bitter cold December 23rd evening in 1949 in the Mt. Zion Methodist Church of Darby, PA. We took advantage of the Christmas holiday vacation during my freshman year at The Thomas Jefferson Medical College and her teaching responsibilities at a nearby suburban public school. Our families considered our timetable to be impetuous, but we began our years together in a low-rent, walk-up third floor apartment located to facilitate the morning and evening commute for each of us. Our parents, pictured above with us, were children of immigrants from England, Scotland, Northern Ireland and Germany. In later years we were drawn by genealogical curiosity to make visits with our children to the homes of aunts, uncles and cousins who remained in the old countries. On those occasions, once relationships were clarified, tears would flow, and the embraces that followed convinced me that "blood is thicker than water".

"Marriage is a public institution that changes people's goals and behaviors by creating obligations and commitments to another. The answer to addressing societal problems resulting from wide-scale divorce is not to declare it 'normal' or just a part of life. The answer must be to restore the primacy and integrity of marriage. That requires changing our cultural mindset that presents marriage as just one of several morally equivalent lifestyle choices. We must elevate marriage to its rightful role as the foundation and backbone of our society."

The intense pleasure that centers on the human reproductive system represents a fertile opportunity for hedonistic exploitation. To what extent does that exploitation contribute to the sexual behavioral disorders that are among the most difficult therapeutic challenges faced by the health care community? Ted Bundy, the serial murderer of countless women and children, confessed before his execution that the readily available pornography of our day contributed mightily to the cultivation of his antisocial behavior. The paraphilias, conditions of sexual arousal by unusual circumstances, are particularly worrisome inasmuch as children and socially destructive practices such as sadism and exhibitionism are involved. These destructive practices are regarded as crimes, and the involvement of law enforcement is usually consequential.

As one who has enjoyed six generations of fine family and as a retired family doctor, I am always profoundly saddened by the fear and anger written on the faces of some young mothers and children when my instinctive friendliness surfaces spontaneously in restaurants and supermarket checkout lines. More than any other problem of our day, the issues of the nuclear family need calm, clinical study and discussion in the best interest of everyone's patriotic hopes.

As you see from this first therapeutic suggestion relating to national embarrassment, society will always be faced with problem solving. That process usually involves personal sacrifice made by many people in the name of what I call patriotism. By "patriotism" I am not referring to a blind, flag-waving exercise, but patriotism that is born of a genuine concern and love for one's nation, a willingness to recognize the siblinghood of all diverse people, and a willingness to sensibly confront, study, and initiate effective solutions for destructive forces that tear at the very fabric of our republic.

Symptomatic therapy is voluntary and self-disciplinary by nature. Elected politicians and church leaders must make a conscious effort to attain high moral standards. Leaders in the business world must overcome the temptations of greed. And the entertainment industry must regain a sense of responsibility for its profound impact on national morale and morality. All of these efforts will favorably affect a grateful citizenry that in and of itself must celebrate unity at the neighborhood level. But always remember, the definitive therapy to be discussed will facilitate our attack on symptoms.

If we are able to make those necessary sacrifices to rediscover patriotic unity, the holidays are in place for the grateful and revitalized celebration of Memorial Day, Veterans Day, and the Fourth of July. I have always been moved by the emotional commitment engendered by our naturalization process and oath. Unfortunately, many of us who were born into this life of liberty accept it apathetically as a matter of entitlement.

Before we leave this first therapeutic suggestion, we should be reminded that many of our diverse differences are rooted in belief systems. The appeal for patriotic unity in no way calls for the abandonment of religious conviction. It is just an appeal to each of us to bring the best that we are to a common table. Our places of worship could be of value in fostering this effort, but it would involve the development of a forum that provides for an interfaith dialogue. Unfortunately many such efforts in the past have lost sight of purpose and break down over sophisticated, esoteric issues that become divisive. It has been the wonderful American experience that people who live side by side with people of other beliefs discover matters of family, friendly, and human commonality that facilitate those sacrifices that are essential for collective social unity.

Chapter XVI

The Relief of Adversarialism

It has been apparent to me that a component of the malaise that has been burdening my patients involved an element of vague interpersonal social anger. By titling this chapter "The Relief of Adversarialism," Anne's computer and Noah Webster have called my attention to the fact that I have coined a new word. I am using "'adversarialism" to identify a process that is designed to cultivate interpersonal animosity.

This interpersonal animosity has infiltrated the worlds of law, medicine, education, industry, politics, and even government. Patients tell me that vocational fulfillment is not what it used to be. Much of this discord has been cultivated for reasons of greed, with unfortunate, alienating consequences between doctors and patients, teachers and students, employers and employees, men and women, the young and the elderly, and, of course, between those with religious and racial differences. During the civilization cycle stages of affluence and greed, Toynbee refers to these manifestations of divisiveness as "schisms." This is most regrettable for an idealistic republic that offered opportunity for all, inspired creativity and ambition, and fostered vocational joy during its first two hundred years.

During my childhood in the first half of the twentieth century, and indeed, when I opened my office in West Chester in 1955, the social helping professions were regarded to be medicine, law, education, and religion. They were dignified and respected. Then, a strange thing happened in this great nation on the way to the twenty-first century. Even though medical science was experiencing unparalleled success in doubling life expectancy, the helping profession of law began to relentlessly attack the helping profession of medicine in the courtroom.

The Honorable Chief Justice Warren Burger noted in 1984 that "there is a litigation neurosis developing in an otherwise normal, well-adjusted people." What Justice Burger did not know was that this neurosis was being carefully nourished by "trial lawyers who pit Americans against each other, so that attorneys can feed on the carnage." This quote comes from the writings of Philip K. Howard, Esq., who published *The Death of Common Sense* in 1996, a book revealing "how law is suffocating America." In 2001 Mr. Howard published *The Collapse of the Common Good*, revealing, "how America's lawsuit culture undermines its own freedom."

In 2003 Robert B. Surrick, Esq., a Chester County attorney, wrote a book explaining the mechanics of the trial lawyers' strategy. As explained and documented by Mr. Surrick, community trial lawyers have been sending large sums of money, represented as dues, to the Pennsylvania Trial Lawyers Association (PATLA) political action committee. This money is used to fund the election campaign coffers of legislators, judges, and governors who favor huge courtroom awards. Then, by virtue of contingency fee contracts, 40 percent to 60 percent of these awards are diverted away from citizen plaintiffs and into the accounts of the trial lawyers.

By originally focusing on neurosurgeons, orthopedic surgeons, and obstetricians, the process has created "high risk" specialties with commensurately exorbitant liability insurance premiums. And where corrective state legislation is nonexistent, because of the special-interest lobbying by the trial lawyers, the process has created "high risk" states. Physician migration, especially among the young, is now a statistical fact. Tort law that exists today fosters fear, greed, and extravagant costs. It focuses on many of our best, highly trained physicians to economically capitalize on the inevitable maloccurrences associated with the diagnostic and therapeutic complexities of humankind's most difficult health problems.

The Chester County Medical Society meets annually with our state and federal elected legislators. Two years ago the physicians pleaded for remedial legislation but were told that legislators will listen when doctors come up with campaign gifts comparable to those of the trial lawyers. What a sad commentary on the evils of special-interest lobbying! And *Newsweek* magazine tells us that there are thirty-five thousand special-interest lobbyists in Washington, D.C. Should not our elected officials be free of economic bribes when determining legislation that is intended to serve the best interest of the citizenry?

I have used the medical predicament because it is best known to me. My broker tells me that a similar scheme exists in the worlds of class action and product liability law. The legal community defends its actions by representing these laws as protection of the public from the faulty products of industry and the potential injurious consequences of professional services. We all agree that these things happen and that injured citizens deserve compensatory consideration if negligence caused the problem. However, the powerful factor of avarice too often leads to extravagance and injustice.

According to Mr. Howard, healthy law should free people to do the right thing. Today, law is so unpredictable that most folks are afraid to do anything. Obstetricians are afraid to deliver babies, neurosurgeons are afraid to operate, clergypersons are afraid to counsel, Little League volunteers are afraid to coach, insurance companies are afraid to write policies, pharmaceutical companies are afraid to manufacture vaccines, and almost every bill we pay is padded by the exorbitant liability expenses of the provider.

Mr. Howard and Mr. Surrick were inspired to write their books because of love of country and a love for their own chosen profession. It is their sincere hope that by a process of reform, law will regain the respect and dignity that it once enjoyed.

And what about the intense, adversarial struggles by our brothers and sisters in the gay community? During my eighty years I have had many of them as good friends and patients. In my experience they are bright, friendly, and often quite talented. Like all of God's children they possess a sense of self-esteem, a thirst for knowledge, a craving for truth and meaning, and a need to love and be loved. Their struggle with society relates to gender identity, a phenomenon that begins at a very young age and may have some roots in genetic predisposition. In our human species, gender recognition and awareness generally occurs in the two- to three-year-old child. For reasons that are still somewhat obscure, the psychological rejection of assigned gender occurs in about one of thirty thousand males and one in about one hundred thousand females.

Young parents not infrequently seek medical attention for behavior, most often cross-dressing, observed in children. My experience has been that these consultations are not motivated by homophobia. Most of these visits are prompted by the profound joy associated with procreation and family life—a fulfilling hope that they have for each of their children. Nevertheless, because of these social concerns, the phenomenon is referred to as "gender identity disorder." The word "disorder" is resented by the gay community; it is a personality characteristic that resists change, and it appears to find fulfillment only in same-sex relationships.

Much of the adversarialism of our day relating to this issue involves the emergence of the nontraditional family. By virtue of adoption and artificial insemination, same-sex couples can have families. As we all know, the social rub arises when demands are made to modify the definition of marriage as we know it, and when educational materials are promoted to advance the nontraditional family as just another option. A majority of the states have rejected laws to allow this.

I have taken time to discuss this issue clinically because of its potential threat to social health and harmony. The conflict between the heterosexual and homosexual communities is rooted in ancient history, and the angry persecution of the minority group is certainly and sadly unjust. Reconfrontation of the subject in recent decades has accomplished great strides in matters of mutual acceptance. Certainly the Christian scripture that provided this nation with its powerful identity is clear about the imperfect nature of each of us. As children of God, nontraditional families need loving inclusion in the human family. I am persuaded that this can be accomplished voluntarily and rationally in the best interest of national patriotism. I am also concerned that a forced solution based on a legal constitutional contest runs the risk of deepening the ancient divide.

Another unfortunate adversarial struggle exists in the world of belief systems. Those who believe that God does not exist take great issue with references to a Creator in our Declaration of Independence. In matters of church-state separation, they press for the deletion of all such references.

The domestic opposition to the concept of a Christian nation during the past half-century has been led by the American Civil Liberties Union, once again a liberal branch from within our own legal family. The ACLU has represented groups that consider Christianity to be superstition at its worst. These groups go by such names as Human Light, Tree of Knowledge, Humanist Association, Atheist Alliance, Secular Coalition for America, and Free Thought Society. According to the Free Thought Society Web site, its beliefs are as follows:

> "Freethought holds that individuals should neither accept nor reject ideas proposed as truth without recourse to knowledge and reason. Thus, freethinkers strive to build their beliefs on the basis of facts, scientific inquiry, and logical principles, independent of

the factual/logical fallacies and intellectually-limiting effects of authority, cognitive bias, conventional wisdom, popular culture, prejudice, sectarianism, tradition, urban legend, and all other dogmatic and fallacious principles."

This adoration of knowledge goes back as far as Socrates (469–399 BC), who taught that only by knowledge could man be virtuous. He and his students Plato and Aristotle were known as philosophers, meaning "lovers of knowledge," or, for some, "lovers of wisdom." It should be noted that humanists and atheists do not have a corner on the love of knowledge. Those who believe in God share that love and possess a compelling desire to use it to serve humankind. There is much common ground between the schools of religion and nonreligion, and accusations of superstition serve only to convey a divisive attitude of condescending derision.

The experiential observation should be made that knowledge is virtue-neutral. Healthy beliefs lead us to use knowledge for virtuous purposes. Conversely, unhealthy beliefs might lead to the use of the same knowledge to support a socially destructive lifestyle. It was the brilliance of Albert Einstein that led us to know that the inert mass of matter possesses the dynamic power of energy. By splitting a single atom, energy can be released that could decimate cities and people therein, or, under controlled circumstances, provide powerful support for education, the arts, industry, and, in general, quality of life. It is the healthy development of the belief systems of human nature that makes the difference.

The previously discussed genetic research of Dr. Francis Collins, our present director of the National Institute of Health, led him from a conviction about the "myth of theism" to a conviction about the "myth of atheism." For Dr. Collins, the synchronous, functioning complexity of the human body, physical universe, and recorded history bespeak evolving meaning unlikely to be accomplished by the fortuitous coincidences of blind physical forces.

For those who find hope, meaning, and inspiration in religious belief, compromise may mean the gracious acceptance of church-state separation as not only a position of fairness, but also as a matter of Christian principle. Nevertheless, each of these two schools of religion and nonreligion are ultimately based on personal belief, and each school should respect the other in this land of free establishment and exercise.

Beyond medicine, law, and religion, adversarialism has penetrated government, politics, and many other aspects of American life. As a destructive force, it fosters the national shame discussed in the previous chapter. Interpersonal anger impedes constructive bipartisan governmental service to the nation. As described by Supreme Court Justice Clark, "The history of man is inseparable from the history of religion, and religion has always been closely identified with our history and government." Truly, behavior and conscience are intimately interrelated at both the individual and national levels.

Paradoxically, diversity has historically been a source of our great national health and strength. As described in the last chapter, our existing friendships with people of other faiths and races suggests that we have a head start on defeating this plague of adversarialism. We must continue to transfuse that asset of diversity with a regulated immigration policy that reflects inclusiveness. And we must develop new and exciting ways to celebrate that diversity.

Chapter XVII

The Relief of Creeping Servitude

During my lifetime the federal government has enacted underfunded, mandatory entitlement programs known as Social Security and Medicare. Everyone from the wealthiest to the poorest must pay into and eventually draw benefits from these programs, whether or not financial help is needed in the golden years. As predicted in the 1930s, the programs are now being drawn on by a huge population that is living longer, and the programs are supported by a working force that is projected to get progressively smaller. In spite of this fiduciary carelessness, the leaders of this great nation are talking about socializing cradle-to-grave health care. The subtle movement of this great nation from a land of liberty toward a land of socialism is probably not very apparent to younger folks, but my poor parents during the Depression were livid about the prospective erosion of an ideal called liberty.

John Stossel, in his syndicated column of June 18, 2008, calls our attention to the fact that Medicare, Medicaid, and Social Security represented 8 percent of the gross domestic product (GDP) in 2007. By virtue of projected population changes, that total will be 14.5 percent in 2030 and 25.7 percent in 2082. To keep pace, tax rates would have to more than double.

The framers of the Constitution were acutely aware of this greatest threat to personal liberty—one's own government. Consequently, they struggled to create a document that would assure the construction and perpetuation of a government that would serve and not rule the people. Dr. Richard Beeman, professor of history at the University of Pennsylvania, assures us that "the Constitution is neither a self-actuating nor a self-correcting document. It requires the constant attention and devotion of all citizens." The document has been amended many times to accomplish, as a constant challenge, "a more perfect union."

With that in mind, I am of the opinion that our "patient USA" is in need of symptomatic relief from a sense of erosion, specifically the erosion of liberty. Professor Beeman tells us that "upon exiting the Constitutional Convention, Benjamin Franklin was asked about the sort of government the delegates had created." Franklin's answer was, "A republic, if you can keep it." Similarly, in 1788, Thomas Jefferson wrote to Carrington, "The natural progress of things is for liberty to yield and for government to gain control."

To clarify the subject being discussed, it should be noted that the word "liberty" evokes a variety of connotations. In this discussion it is used to simply denote "the quality or state of being free" (Webster). It does not mean "the power or right to do as one pleases." This latter concept, promoted by some folks, is the source of many of the problems of today—"you can't discipline me; I know my rights!" Solzhenitsyn refers to this very evident Western trait as "the decadence of irresponsible freedom."

I am convinced that the general public does have a vague feeling that liberty is being eroded, and that the government is gaining more and more control. From my waiting-room conversations, barbershop small talk, and retirement community table talk, I hear such questions, as:

1. Did not our founding fathers, in the name of liberty, believe that government should be only large enough to do for people what people could not do for themselves?

2. Why do we, as citizens, love benefits but hate taxes? Should not social programs be presented with a very clear explanation of the cost and the means of financing?

3. Is it not true that a nation's strength is best judged by the care that it provides for its weakest members—the young, the elderly, and the sick who are poor?

4. Have we not proven that expensive, underfunded entitlement legislation spreads the benefits over so large a group that the truly needy are often underserved?

5. Why is government such a poor manager of business? Is it wise to finance expensive programs with federal bond issues, often bought up by nations whose friendship is uncertain? And, should we be passing huge national debt on to our children and grandchildren, or should not the eradication of national debt be expected of our elected officials?

6. Should interminable political careers be allowed, or might term limits and fresh faces from the world of industry and other professions reduce extravagant governmental inefficiency?

7. How much of our governance is actually determined by our elected officials and how much is the product of a huge, permanent, expensive bureaucracy?

8. Are my elected officials really serving me, or are their decisions influenced by the money of special-interest lobbying groups?

9. Should unrelated earmark riders, solely designed as "pork" to assure reelection, be allowed as tag-ons for good proposed legislation?

10. In view of human need, should we not insist on political campaign reform to assure fairness as well as the conservation of millions of dollars?

In 1979 Anne and I traveled with a delegation from the Pennsylvania Medical Society to study socialized medicine in a free nation, Sweden, and a Communist dictatorship, the Union of Soviet Socialist Republics (USSR). This was during the Cold War and before the "wall" came down. At the end of the tour, my seatmate on our flight from Moscow to Vienna turned out to be an economist from Luxembourg, who listened with interest to my observations. In Sweden the doctors were doing well financially but were unhappy with the government's domination of health care decisions. Our Swedish bus driver was unhappy because so many of the young people were "off on carefree holiday much of the time—swimming down in the Canary Islands." In Russia, health care was primitive and was delivered through "polyclinics," each with an identical construction plan and scattered evenly through the cities of Leningrad and Moscow. The overwhelming memory of each member of our entourage on that flight related to the fear and sadness written on the faces of Soviet citizens. We each felt a sense of relief as we left that nation. Yet, in spite of Soviet poverty and high 80 percent to 90 percent Swedish income taxes, patriotism in both countries prompted its citizens to proudly claim that education and health care are "free."

My new friend, the Luxembourg economist, explained that governmental paternalism destroys initiative, ambition, creativity, and meaning in life. Unfortunately, it fosters boredom and alcoholism, problems in both of those nations. The government becomes all things to all people, and voluntarism is an unknown concept.

Perhaps there is no one more poorly prepared to comment on economic matters than a physician. After walking across the stage at the Philadelphia Academy of Music to receive my Jefferson diploma in 1953, I was suddenly faced with the need to operate a small business with matters of income, expenses, and product quality. I had a young and growing family to protect and necessarily interfaced with the world of health and life insurance. By virtue of the small business, I necessarily explained to my government each year matters of accountability relating to civic taxation. And when, after many years, I realized something called "discretionary income," I began to concern myself with another discipline called investments and retirement planning. This whole economic process for me was a matter of learn-as-you-go, work hard for your family and patients, and curiously endeavor to understand the good and the bad features of the free enterprise system.

To convey a feel for how far we've come in fifty years, the first patient to arrive in my waiting room on August 5, 1955, paid me $3.00 for services rendered. In those days I was paid $5.00 for house calls and $1.50 for each welfare patient. By October 16, 1955, things were beginning to gain momentum, and by virtue of a nine-patient caseload, I recorded a $39.00 income for the day! I am glad that I kept some of those old records and can cite them now to reflect the truth that health care costs were least expensive when fee-for-service transactions were accomplished with doctor-to-patient eye contact on the spot.

So here we are at the beginning of the twenty-first century, still trying to make sense of the economic behavior of society. It has been said that "God invented economists to make weathermen feel better about themselves." I cite that now to insult neither of those fine professionals, but to call our attention to the variable nature of the geologic forces and sociological moods upon which prediction is so often unreliably dependent.

Every visitor to the Constitution Center in Philadelphia is reminded that we are living in a nation where the power resides in the people. This chapter is written to illuminate the most important decision of this moment. Do we want to keep the republic so carefully crafted by our foreparents, or do we want to surrender personal liberty to creeping socialism?

The constitutional intent of our founding fathers is clearly revealed in the words of Franklin and Jefferson. With the power vested in the people, a small, elected, representative government was intended to serve them, and the protection of personal liberty was assured to motivate them. The role of small government was defined to provide for its citizens what they could not provide for themselves—national defense and security, public education, a mail service, a highway network, and care for the poor.

The specific intent of this defined role was to keep the government out of business. The free enterprise consequence of the plan was to competitively keep product excellence high, expenses low, and prices reasonable. This system has proven to stimulate creativity and ambition with a resultant standard of living heretofore unknown in history.

The problem with governmental involvement in business has always been the absence of need for accountability. There is no competitive motive to keep expenses low, costs low, and profits high—tax income can always be raised to balance the books, or the national debt can be expanded by borrowing. There is also no competitive reason to strive for product excellence. Hence, the valid cliché that "the government is run like nobody's business."

It has been said that a government plan to provide health care for all would probably have the monetary appetite of the Defense Department, the efficiency of the Post Office, and the compassion of the IRS. For those in politics who criticize the rising cost of health care, it is interesting to note that spending by the federal government grew from 3 percent of the gross domestic product (GDP) in 1925 to 15.6 percent in 1950. In its *125 Year Picture of the Federal Government Share of the Economy*, our Congressional Budget Office (CBO) goes on to project that this cost will rise to 20.8 percent in 2020, 26.9 percent in 2050, and 36.5 percent in 2070. This predicted relentless drift into economic bondage is the result of known population projections, mandated sociological entitlement programs, and the payment of interest (debt service) on the money borrowed by our government to create this economic monster.

Perhaps this chart constructed by our own Congressional Budget Office will best reflect the cost of our socialized, entitlement programs since 1950, as will their projected costs until the year 2075.

A 125-year Picture of the Federal Government's Share of the Economy, 1950 to 2075, as percentage of GDP.							
Fiscal Year	Social Security	Medicare	Medicaid	Social Security, Medicare and Medicaid Combined	All Other Spending, Excluding Interest Expenses	Interest Expenses	Total
1950	0.3%	n.a	n.a	0.3%	13.5%	1.8%	15.6%
1960	2.2%	n.a	n.a	2.2%	14.2%	1.3%	17.7%
1962	2.5%	n.a	n.a	2.5%	15.1%	1.2%	18.8%
1970	2.9%	0.7%	0.3%	3.9%	12.8%	1.4%	19.3%
1980	4.3%	1.2%	0.5%	6.0%	13.7%	1.9%	21.6%
1990	4.3%	1.9%	0.7%	6.9%	11.7%	3.2%	21.8%
2000	4.2%	2.2%	1.2%	7.6%	8.5%	2.3%	18.4%
2010	4.4%	2.7%	1.8%	8.8%	7.6%	0.8%	17.2%
2020	5.4%	3.6%	2.3%	11.3%	7.1%	-0.5%	17.9%
2030	6.2%	4.9%	2.8%	13.9%	7.1%	-0.2%	20.8%
2040	6.2%	6.0%	3.4%	15.5%	7.1%	1.1%	23.8%
2050	6.0%	6.7%	3.9%	16.7%	7.1%	3.1%	26.9%
2060	6.1%	7.7%	4.3%	18.1%	7.1%	5.8%	31.0%
2070	6.2%	8.9%	4.9%	20.0%	7.1%	9.4%	36.5%
2075	6.2%	9.6%	5.3%	21.1%	7.1%	11.5%	39.7%

This chart was constructed by the Congressional Budget Office in 2002. It does not take into account that the cost of government in 2009 was the highest in our nation's history – a whopping 61.34 percent of our GDP. As a result of that year, our annual Cost of Government Day fell on August 12, 23 days later than ever before! Consequently, to reflect our present and exploding national debt, columns seven and eight deserve upward revision.

Unfortunately, politicians take advantage of human nature by promising governmental gifts with underestimated cost projections. They are making these offers to a populace that, by virtue of human nature, adores free gifts, but, by virtue of historical experience, hates taxes. This relentless process is drawing us subtly away from the intended conservative republic and toward the liberal state of socialism abhorred by our nation's founders.

Bill and Melinda Gates have shown us all that fiscal responsibility and mandated accountability, as practiced in the real world of business, can be effectively applied to the alleviation of third-world suffering. This kind of leadership in governmental spending is sorely needed. In connection with the exemplary philanthropy of the Gateses and so many other benefactors in American history, it should be noted that generosity and voluntarism are unique consequences of our nation's religious and governmental philosophic legacy. Indeed, the survival of the free enterprise system is dependent on empathy and spontaneous giving. George Will, in his syndicated column of March 27, 2008, points out "that religion is the single biggest predictor of a person's altruism. America is largely divided between religious givers and secular nongivers, and the former are disproportionately conservative."

This chapter on creeping servitude has turned out to be unreasonably economic in content. Perhaps this has happened because of the fiscal path that we have voluntarily selected as a nation. Is it possible, as Toynbee suggests, that economic suicide driven by greed is subtly leading us back into a state of apathetic government bondage? Or, as our historian suggests, is it possible for us to demand the painful, corrective legislation from the government that we employ—legislation that will eliminate national debt, restore the spiritual creativity of prior generations, and open the doors to loftier achievements not yet envisioned?

Certainly the quality of life enjoyed by the masses of people in this great nation provides evidence for a successful outcome of the social experiment discussed in chapter 12. To that consideration we must add the happiness associated with fulfillment in all aspects of human nature that is provided by this land of liberty. It is hard to believe that we would consider any other course of action, but there are those who see bigger government as the road to an even better life. Unfortunately, history suggests that this line of reasoning rejects inspired idealism and too often leads to the meaningless mediocrity of secularism.

Chapter XVIII

Definitive Therapy

So, what can an old, country, family doctor do about a health problem that he has seen gradually develop, and for which, in his opinion, there is a cure? By now, he has probably been disregarded by his own profession for the anecdotal nature of his uncontrolled study. And he has undoubtedly alienated other readers into whose territory he has wandered with his expanded definition of health. Is it possible that this whole treatise is about a great nation that, by virtue of the growing pains of the past sixty years, is becoming even greater?

West Chester is a beautiful, small college town lying in the rolling Brandywine Valley hills of Pennsylvania's Chester County. The town and county enjoy high rates of education, income, and recreational opportunity with low rates of unemployment. It is interesting to discover when you are working on a project of this kind how paradoxical observations leap off pages, but last Sunday, in our packed Presbyterian sanctuary, I read the following bulletin announcement:

"*Mothers Group* will meet on Wednesday, April 16, from 9:30 a.m. until 11 a.m. in rooms 407 and 408. *This Week: Mr. Stewart's Self-Defense.* Learn some basic moves to protect yourself and your little ones if you are ever in an unfortunate situation. Wear comfortable clothes! Child care is available."

George Will, in his syndicated column of June 22, 2008, reports that the studies by Heather MacDonald of the Manhattan Institute reveal that between 1998 and 2004, violent offenders accounted for all of the increase in our growing prison population. Don't tell me that the concerns that I am addressing are fictitious. For reasons unknown, it is a fact that human beings have the uncivilized capacity for unbelievable cruelty. As mentioned during our discussion of goodness and badness, one needs only to look at the Adolf Hitlers, Joseph Stalins, Ted Bundys or the daily news media of the twenty-first century. On the other hand, the Albert Schweitzers, Mother Teresas, and Irena Sendlers of history have left records of selfless goodness and service. Systems of belief can powerfully motivate behavior of all kinds.

In answer to the question posed above, an old, country, family doctor concerned about his own "sweet land of liberty" has the right and responsibility, by God (a nonprofane literalism), to speak up. At my age there is no time for triple-blind, multicentric studies, so anecdotes will have to do.

As well-trained physicians, we have initiated measures to provide symptomatic relief. We know that these measures will be palliative and that the relief will be transient, at best. And we know that, without a definitive, curative ingredient, relapse will be an almost certain consequence. The fact that I am still writing and that you are still reading suggests that we share a love for our patient, the United States of America. Don't underestimate the importance of that dimension, for it is at the heart of what Hippocrates called "the art of the practice."

During the past half century, I have watched my sweet land of liberty wrestle desperately with the social and emotional symptoms discussed in the previous three chapters. During my retiring years of reflection, I have become increasingly suspicious that our national decline of wellness can be best understood at its deepest level as a spiritual crisis.

This discussion of a cure is at the very center of this book's purpose. The miracle measure for which we search must deal in a logical way with all of the other previously discussed facts relating to our history, physical examination, special studies, tentative diagnosis, and therapeutic plan. The miracle measure must deal with the emotional malaise, our patient's chief complaint; it must deal with our nation's behavioral deterioration—with issues of pride, affluence, and apathy; it must deal with the consequences of our successes—increasing diversity; and, it must involve a consideration of our diverse belief systems, that aspect of each human's nature that profoundly impact mood, values, and social accord.

Such a miracle measure with these intimidating goals would appear to be beyond our wildest dream, but that was once said about infectious diseases. Having started this treatise with a rehearsal of Memorial Day in the 1930s, my mind has again drifted back to the simplicity of childhood in search for such a remedy.

While I was still in grade school, my parents introduced me to the "shorter catechism" of our church. Our friend Noah Webster defines "catechism" as "a summary of religious doctrine, often in the form of questions and answers." As a little kid, the commitment of answers to memory was a piece of cake. Understanding religious doctrine, the profundity of most of the canned answers, and their relationship to the development of a personal belief system were quite beyond me. I can only remember a sense of gratitude for the brevity of the assignment—after all, the title "shorter catechism" implied that there must be a longer one that I was not being called upon to memorize.

Interestingly, the only question that I can still remember was the first: "What is the chief end of man?" As a child, the only chief I knew about related to our favorite game of cowboys and Indians. And the only ends of man apparent to me were his upper and lower. Nevertheless, this question was my father's favorite, and he repeatedly hammered it home. The spoon-fed answer that we kids learned to regurgitate at any moment's notice was, "The chief end of man is to glorify God and to enjoy him forever."

Perhaps this is a moment of defensive paranoia for me, but I can hear it now: "Doctor, that is the dumbest, most abstract, most irrelevant suggestion that I have ever heard! As a person representing a discipline that has uncovered so much truth scientifically, and as one who has described well many of our twenty-first century practical problems, are you implying that the most important purpose in life, and indeed, as our definitive solution, that we must learn to 'glorify God'?"

In response to that rhetorical question, let me only say that for decades patients have told me, and for centuries people have testified to the effect that, "It works." The consequences of the experience are described as fulfillment, happiness, and social accord. Further, this was not my or the church's good idea. One of history's greatest teachers, Christ himself, was asked by religious scholars and secular lawyers about the most important law on the books. His reply was to the effect that the first law, "to love the Lord your God with all your heart, soul, and mind" was of greatest importance and represented the underlying basis for all other laws.

As mentioned at the beginning of our therapeutics discussion, a loving, cooperative mood is basically conducive to concessions by adversarial parties in search of constructive solutions. The "spiritual creativity" described by Mr. Toynbee during the formative years of any young social unit gives rise to the industrious accomplishment of comfort, happiness, and pride. The adversarial schisms described by him in times of affluence are the consequence of "spiritual demoralization" voluntarily adopted by the greed-driven, self-centered members of the group. Fortunately, if the society comes to its senses, the powerful ingredient of spiritual creativity can be recaptured.

As therapists, when powerful claims are made about any definitive modality, we are entitled to ask, "What is the nature of the proposed remedy? How does it work? Why is it effective?" Let us explore those questions about glorification.

What is "glorification," and what role does it play in the recovery of wholeness?

Noah Webster defines "glorification" as the decision to "extol because of magnificence." I strongly suspect that our understanding of the word has become narrowed by the repetition of common practice and the passage of time. We associate the exercise with a holy day, the use of ceremonies, prayers, and musical glorias and doxologies that "praise God from whom all blessings flow." But scripture instructs us that ultimate glorification is not just an institutional, one-day-a-week ritual...it is a way of living. It is this understanding of the word that delivers its application from that of abstract irrelevance to that of practical value for the faltering health of a great nation.

True glorification in its fullest sense is expressed in lives that aggressively seek goodness in matters of family, vocation, environment, economics, recreation, art, and civil patriotism. What would be the nature of a nation if improving physical health was accompanied by a citizenry committed to lives of comprehensive doxology?

First of all, the glorification of God by our nation in the twenty-first century would restore the identity described by our founders in our Declaration of Independence. It would reaffirm the evident truths about ourselves as creatures with the capacity to conceptualize, hope for, and believe in a Creator. It would reaffirm our conviction that a good Creator exists who regards each of us to be of equal value and who has blessed us with unalienable human rights. And it would instill in each of us a sense of gratitude.

Although that Declaration of Independence was written in the predominant context of Christian Protestantism, it has always occurred to me that the most significant force responsible for one's belief system is the family into which one is born. And over that event, no one has control. Inasmuch as gratitude to one's Creator is a common theme among most religions, and in the presence of increasing national diversity, is it conceivable that, in an effort to recapture the thrust of that Declaration, a year of glorification could be celebrated in the churches, synagogues, temples, mosques, meetinghouses, and homes of the United States of America? Beyond its value to the restoration of our identity, what would this say to the world about the Fatherhood of God and the siblinghood of humankind? And what would it say to the true church in the name of longed-for ecumenism? Is there not a Christian hymn that suggests "There's a Wideness in God's Mercy"? That hymn proclaims that "there's a kindness in His justice, which is more than liberty."

How does glorification work to restore wholeness?

The forthright claim of the first question in our catechism is to the effect that glorification is the chief end of each person. In contrast to my juvenile understanding of "chiefs" and "ends," my theological friends have explained to me that "ends" are really values or purposes. The scriptural claim is that when we glorify God as the central purpose in life, all other values derive relative meaning and fall into place—family, vocation, wealth, the arts, recreation, and just good old-fashioned self-serving pursuits.

Glorification, as an abstraction, translates into practical social action through the powerful, motivating force of gratitude. Medically speaking, there is a complementary and interdependent relationship between the three symptomatic, voluntary, therapeutic measures previously discussed and this definitive therapeutic suggestion. People who are grateful for God's graceful generosity work aggressively and voluntarily on matters of national shame, seek ways to express neighborliness to overcome adversarialism, and jealously protect the liberty of their republic. In the alleviation of symptoms we find that the recovery of religious identity is both facilitated and facilitatory.

In his children's book *The Secret of Saying Thanks*, Douglas Wood asks, "Are people thankful because they are happy or happy because they are thankful?" Just after Christmas, I asked this question of the second-graders to whom I read and was surprised by the philosophic discussion that erupted among the eight-year-olds. Wood's point is that thankful people are usually happy—a best-kept secret!

The Four Poole Daughters (1961). The concept of a loving, creator God engenders gratitude for all of life's gifts...parents, talents, siblings, education, nature, vocation and recreation. Foremost among these belongs the joy of parenthood. During the 1950's Anne and I were blessed by the arrival of four wonderful daughters: Pamela, Cynthia, Kristina and Melissa. To this day they remain loving good friends, continue to rehearse amusing childhood memories, and have expanded the nuclear family with five treasured grandchildren.

The benefits of gratitude are not just psychological trickery. According to Robert A. Emmons, Ph.D., professor of psychology at the University of California, Davis, the lives of people who are grateful are measurably healthier and qualitatively better than those dominated by envy, resentment, and regret. People who give thanks to God and other fellow human beings are "happier, have longer more loving marriages, have more successful careers, have annual salaries $25,000 higher than unhappy college graduates sixteen years after graduation, are physically healthier, and live an average of seven to nine years longer than chronically unhappy persons." This 2005 analysis of hundreds of psychological studies supports the here-and-now benefits of interest to my medical theology. I do not advocate the pursuit of religion for self-serving reasons, but it is encouraging to know that the gratitude of a healthy belief system is constantly buffering us from the counterproductive emotions of pessimism, envy, resentment, and regret.

Glorification—why does it work to restore wholeness?

Cardinal Anthony Joseph Bevilacqua, the archbishop of Philadelphia between 1987 and 2003, was asked this question during a televised news conference, and I heard him say, "For those who believe, no explanation is necessary, and for those who don't, no explanation is ever enough." The cardinal's point was that religion is personally experiential. For centuries people have testified to the discovery of meaning in life, comfort in times of distress, and fulfillment with regard to the human need to love and to be loved.

During a recent interview by the Reverend Rick Warren at the Saddleback Church in California, Senator John McCain, the 2008 U.S. presidential candidate, was asked about the personal meaning of his own Christian faith. Senator McCain's succinct reply was, "the assurance of forgiveness, redemption, and salvation." This initiative by God through Jesus Christ is the very central claim of the Christian religion and represents the foundation for the here-and-now medical theology discussed in this book.

The Judeo-Christian understanding of man's rebellious separation from God and the subsequent ongoing struggle for reconciliation was factually evident to Saint Paul in his letter to Rome and is evident to many who honestly examine themselves. The "why it works" scriptural explanation involves God's spirit working through those who have accomplished that vertical reconciliation. The compelling desire to be "an instrument of his peace," to quote Saint Francis, is described by folks in many different ways, but the contemplation of a master plan is fascinating, historically reassuring, and compatible with belief in an omnipotent, loving Creator, who has the "whole world in His hands."

Glorification—the remedy of choice

Having discussed the what, how, and why relating to the therapeutic efficacy of the glorification of God, let us say a few words about the selection of this remedy of choice. Since the discovery of penicillin in middle of the last century, medical and pharmaceutical research has developed a whole host of new antibiotic families and family members. When treating infectious diseases, physicians usually culture the causative organism and perform antibiotic, laboratory, sensitivity studies before selecting the drug of choice. This careful search for a specific remedy most commonly leads to the hoped-for, patient-centered, curative results.

In the best interest of the malaise, embarrassment, adversarialism, and eroded liberty of our "patient USA," our diagnostic assessment suggests that, at the deepest level, a faltering belief system is causative. Consequently, our remedy of choice is selectively designed to effect cure. Is it possible that the technological accomplishments of the twentieth century, including computers, prolongation of life, and genome manipulation, have led us into a delusional state of self-sufficiency? And, if so, might we, in our affluence, be proudly munching on the Eden apple of the twenty-first century?

A republic is a wonderful concept of government, but as a fragile civic ideal, Franklin and Jefferson were frankly pessimistic about its chances for survival as an instrument of, by, and for the people. The evolution of a republic toward "a more perfect union" is dependent on the goodness of the people. To accomplish goodness, the rule of law is certainly necessary, but it is reactive in nature and not likely to effect cure. In accordance with the principles of therapy as taught by Dr. Rehfus, our nation's needs are for a solution that is proactive and definitively effective.

As a matter of interesting coincidence, while writing this chapter, the death of Alexander Solzhenitsyn on August 3, 2008, at the age of eighty-nine was reported in our local newspaper. As mentioned before, this Nobel Prize-winning Russian author had suffered eight years of Soviet gulag imprisonment because of his conscientious objection to the socialism and communism of Lenin and Stalin. Solzhenitsyn loved the United States of America and opined that its strength resided in its religious integrity. He stated that the West will fall if it ever turns its back on its strength in faith. He was invited to speak at Harvard University in 1978 and shocked the audience by expressing concern about Western decadence already in progress in the context of American affluence. Cal Thomas, in his syndicated column of August 8, 2008, points out that Alexander's critique rings even more true today, when measured by "cable television programming that is filled with the vain, the vulgar, and the vacuous."

The phrase "God bless America" is so often mouthed that it is rarely thought of as Irving Berlin's prayer motivated by gratitude:

> While the storm clouds gather
>
> Far across the sea,
>
> Let us swear allegiance
>
> To a land that's free.
>
> Let us all be grateful
>
> For a land so fair,
>
> As we raise our voices
>
> In a solemn prayer.

God bless America,
Land that I love.
Stand beside her,
And guide her,
Through the night
With a light from above.
From the mountains to the prairies
To the oceans white with foam,
God Bless America, my home sweet home,
God Bless America, my home sweet home.

The value of glorification as a proactive, remedial measure is based on my understanding of human nature. Some will certainly disagree with all of my reasoning and suggestions, and it is commendable that we are each free to do so. Critics are quick to rehearse episodes of evil behavior enacted in the name of religion. And the media, too, often depict religious activity and beliefs as those exemplified by the Jonestown mass suicide, Nazi master-race genocide, Crusade violence, cowardly terrorism, or exercises in financial exploitation. These are examples of humankind's manipulation of religion, and they have understandably embittered many. It is important to realize that the vast majority of the world's and this nation's devout abide by a moderate and honest understanding of scriptural teaching.

This chapter on definitive therapy reflects on the meaning of the "medical theology" that I have referred to in this book. Physicians are fact and results oriented, and all of us should have an interest in the therapeutic value of theistic glorification. In a very practical fashion, the social seasoning of reverence can only favorably impact our twenty-first century problems of embarrassment, adversarialism, and loss of liberty. The restoration of healthy self-esteem and patriotic pride will go far to get our poor old Uncle Sam back on his feet.

❖ ❖ ❖

Chapter XIX

As a Matter of Fact...

This commonly used phrase is at the heart of all scientific curiosity. And much has been accomplished by honest investigative research during the past 150 years to convert unknowns to theory and theory to fact.

As a grade-school student growing up in the Depression of the 1930s, I can still remember wishing for a new red bicycle with balloon tires and a handle-bar basket—just like those owned by rich kids! When I asked my thrifty mother and grandmother why they followed me around the house turning lights out, their standard answer usually included, "As a matter of fact, Bobby, the sooner you learn to turn out lights not in use, the sooner you will have that red bike with balloon tires and a handle-bar basket."

These were my first lessons in logic, and implied were some factual, unspoken premises that included:

- Electricity costs money.
- Wasted electricity increases the family cost of living.
- Increased cost of living reduces discretionary dollars.
- Bicycles are extravagances that are purchased with discretionary assets.

Not until I got into my undergraduate studies at Ursinus College did I take a course called Logic 101—and it was taught by my most admired professor, Dr. Charles Mattern. I was to discover that the sound reasoning of logic was a discipline of philosophy, intimately related to the subject matter of the sciences and the humanities.

Now that I am up in years, the discipline is most often called upon as it relates to memory. When Anne asks me if I have seen her glasses, my standard reply is, "Where were you when you last used them?" Not infrequently, her response includes, "As a matter of fact, I was in the kitchen this morning trying to read one of your mother's old recipes."

The subject of fact brings me back to *The Language of God*, the fine book written by Dr. Francis S. Collins, the present director of the National Institutes of Health and the past director of the Human Genome Project. In that book, Dr. Collins reviews matters of fact that have been discovered in the sciences of astronomy, physics, chemistry, biology, geology, and fossils, all of which evoke a sense of awe and all of which might support the possible existence of a Creator. His bench work in the laboratory and his patient care at the bedside have led him to conclude that science and spirituality are complementary, and a deepened appreciation of both are needed to comprehend wholeness in its fullest sense.

The doctor's conclusion is that "the God of the Bible is also the God of the genome. He can be worshiped in the cathedral or in the laboratory. His creation is majestic, awesome, intricate, and beautiful—and it cannot be at war with itself. Only we imperfect humans can start such battles. And only we can end them."

As a matter of personal testimony, Dr. Collins reminds each reader that "life is short. The death rate will be one per person for the foreseeable future. Opening one's self to the life of the spirit can be indescribably enriching. Don't put off a consideration of these questions of eternal significance until some personal crisis or advancing age forces the recognition of spiritual impoverishment."

In contrast to Dr. Collins's reasoning from the scientific aspects of the universe, my experiences in the family practice of medicine have led me to consider a presence of God from the health value aspect of belief systems. Regardless of the approach, I think that both of us conclude that history is favorably affected by the human belief in a Creator's existence.

As a retired physician, I am acutely aware of the fact that circumstantial writing often obscures an intended conclusion. The reader often wonders, "Doctor, what's your point?" As I finish this nineteenth chapter and contemplate writing three more, I am reminded of the huge number of monthly medical journals that land on physicians' desks and on medical library shelves. I always had a stack of reading to catch up on, a visible guilt trip, and a clutter that I expect was dealt with by my family on trash day, when I was at the office.

Medical journal articles always begin with statistical data, bench and patient trial research data, a section on interpretation, and, always, a concluding summary to make the point. I strongly suspect that, as do some last-chapter recreational readers, many physicians read the concluding summary first to discover the purpose of the author. They then may delve into the study's methodology, if the point to be made relates to their own personal work. And heaven help the author if, during the scientific research, he or she has fudged the data to make a spectacular claim. Physicians are trained to read critically.

With that commitment to our honest search for truth in mind, let me concisely state the reasoning that has given rise to this book's concern for our nation:

1. If goodness were instinctive, there would be no greed, crime, or unhappiness.

2. During the past sixty years, evidence has suggested that greed, crime, and unhappiness appear to be on the increase.

3. The conceptualization of God is universally instinctive.

4. Hope for God's existence and life's meaning is shared by most individuals.

5. Belief in God is elective. We are creatures of free will.

6. Belief begets humility—the natural consequence of the concept of Creator, creation, and creature.

7. Humility begets gratitude—all blessings are gifts.

8. Gratitude begets pervasive glorification—in all aspects of life.

9. Collective glorification begets collective goodness.

10. Collective goodness begets collective greatness.

The most determinative step in this progressive sequence is to be found in conscious decision number five, for we, as agents of free will, seem possessed by the human insistence that seeing is believing. Bertrand Russell (1872–1971) was a brilliant mathematical logician who received the Nobel Prize for Literature in 1951. By applying the principles of logic to history, psychology, and sociology, he concluded that humankind does not have free will, that religion is responsible for all of the world's misfortunes, and that, for claiming deity and allowing evil, Jesus Christ was immoral. He believed that God does not exist, that people are devoid of intrinsic value, and that life, as an experience defined by birth and death, has no meaning beyond self-realization.

Russell's writing can be better understood in the context of his birth into old English aristocracy, his father's commitment to and writings in support of atheism, the loss of his parents before he became five years old, a desperately lonely childhood, and the foster-parent influence of his grandparents, a lord and lady. His grandmother embraced a brand of Victorian Christianity that forbade sweet desserts, children's play in the village, warm baths twelve months a year, and card playing on Sunday for fear the practice would be seen by the eight servants of the home. His writings on life's meaninglessness resulted in numerous conflicts with society of that day and a domestic record of three failed marriages.

Nevertheless, motivated by humanitarian concerns, in 1963 Russell formed an international body for seeking peaceful solutions, the Bertrand Russell Peace Foundation, which included in its list of sponsors such eminent individuals as Albert Schweitzer, Linus Pauling, Max Born, and Prime Minister Nehru. During his final years, he took up the cause of political prisoners in Brazil, Burma, the Congo, Greece, the Philippines, Iraq, and Russia. After the assassination of President John Kennedy, Russell headed the British "Who Killed Kennedy" Committee, which denounced the Warren Commission report as a massive cover-up. The gentleman was a brilliant enigma.

Karl Marx referred to the religious aspect of human nature as an "opiate of the people," and many continue to write it off as myth. As a physician, my objective, clinical emphasis rests upon the fact that belief systems and free will are just factual aspects of human nature. My observation is that all people make conscious decisions to believe something, and then we quietly go about the business of living accordingly. None of us can prove to anyone else the absolute validity of whatever that position happens to be.

It is for that reason that we must rely on observed results in our study of values. It was the Christian understanding of spiritual liberty that gave rise to our experiment with civil liberty. That concept has given rise to a process that has brought out the best in people during our first, formative two hundred years. During the past half century we appear to have lost sight of concept and process with the consequential, unfortunate "trade of sacred birthright for a mess of pottage." With regard to the needs of our day and our nation, I am of the opinion that the definitive measure described in the previous chapter will facilitate the alleviation of embarrassment, adversarialism, and servitude, and put us back on the road to wholeness.

Consequently, having described our new president as a devout family man, I now place great value on that first adjective, "devout." To recover our identity as a Christian nation, a reverent first family in our White House would offer priceless power to our collective hope.

Section Five

Preventive Medicine

Chapter XX

A Stitch in Time Saves Nine

No medical therapeutic discussion would be complete without an observation regarding the importance of preventive medicine. More important than the symptomatic and definitive therapeutic measures designed to treat illness, prevention is by far the more desirable goal. In 1799 a British physician by the name of Edward Jenner noted that milkmaids were spared when lethal epidemics of smallpox would sweep through Europe. He observed cowpox lesions on the hands of these laboring maids and wondered if those vesicles played a protective role.

With that in mind he took an orphaned boy from a London street corner and scratched some cowpox pus into the boy's arm. A month later he scratched some smallpox pus into the other arm, and Jamie Phipps, the first person subjected to successful immune system manipulation by a safe vaccine, did not get sick. Our therapeutic parallel, of course, suggests that the establishment of a healthy belief system at a young age can serve as a reliable foundation for a lifetime of wellness. I tell my friends in public health that they receive too little credit, for that which is prevented is rarely appreciated.

Jamie Phipps was protected from smallpox for the rest of his life. From that experience we developed a host of preventive vaccines, and most young parents follow an immunization schedule carefully designed by the American Academy of Pediatrics to protect their children. During my childhood we all had whooping cough, and my own sister almost died from diphtheria, but DPT (diphtheria, pertussis, tetanus) vaccine has changed all of that. In my many years of medical practice, I did see a few cases of pertussis (whooping cough), but never a case of tetanus or diphtheria, still killers in third-world countries.

If, indeed, in the best interest of their nation, young families would return to the chief end of man, healthy belief systems in children would become established during their formative years. The cultivated gratitude for all of God's good gifts could only impact ambition, behavior, and happiness favorably, and for generations to come the preservation of liberty within a great republic would be assured.

Ultimately, conscience modifies (or fails to modify) the aggressive drives that are responsible for human behavior. My oldest daughter worked as a probation officer in the Juvenile Probation Office of Chester County for ten years in the 1980s. Much of her work related to the transporting of delinquent children from courthouses to juvenile detention centers. And much of that transportation time provided for one-on-one conversations in the absence of lawyers and judges. Interestingly, many of these children honestly did not understand that what they had done was wrong. Her trips often involved siblings from the same families, and ultimately left Pam with a sense of hopelessness. Conscience is acquired, not inherited.

Our public schools are the logical institutions for the cultivation of healthy citizenship. That's where the young minds of diversity are brought together. In the second-grade classes to which I have been reading during my twelve-year retirement, my young American audience is always of evident African, Caucasian, Oriental, and Hispanic descent. Without endorsing a specific belief system, there is no reason why these young minds could not learn about the anatomy of the human personality, the republic's dependence on goodness for survival, and the ultimate siblinghood of humankind.

However, if our public schools are to be forbidden to teach wholeness, we must do a better job with religious education in our homes and religious institutions during our children's early years. They will then carry these healthy ideas into the classroom and provide educational benefits for peers and social benefits for the nation.

With that in mind, it occurs to me that I did not finish the Clyde Leaver story. You may recall that I worked as a Rotary fundraiser between 1986 and 1988 to pay for the immunization of third-world children against polio. By some strange coincidence, in 1988 my own church, the Westminster Presbyterian Church of West Chester, was concerned about its center-city, land-locked circumstance involving a lack of parking, handicapped access, and air conditioning. The congregation felt that the work of church mission was hopelessly compromised at that location.

With much trepidation, relocation of the church to the edge of town was agreed upon, and with a leap of faith the move was accomplished using in-house skills of congregational members. I used my own fundraising experience to conduct five three-year-pledge capital fund drives, and at the end of the fifteen years (1992–2007), the $8.5 million project was paid for, the congregation had more than doubled in size, and Presbyterian Homes was planning to surround the church with a CCRC (continuing care retirement community).

In 1988 the congregation of the Westminster Presbyterian Church of West Chester, PA numbered about 1100 members. The congregation possessed the vital desire to be mission driven – with a particular focus on its home community and social needs crying for attention. Collectively, the church recognized physical problems that limited mission effectiveness, and in 1992, relocated the edifice in which the church meets. The new meeting place, pictured here, has effectively accomplished results far beyond our most optimistic hopes.

I go back to that story because of a desire to describe our church's five-day-per-week Christian preschool that serves over two hundred children each year. The building is booming with activity seven days a week, the ethical and academic head start for the children is coveted by the young families of our community, and this aspect of mission was quite unforeseen.

I have attended some of those preschool graduations, have heard the testimonies of these little ones, and feel personally rewarded by the social impact of this aspect of church mission. It bodes well for the future.

As Supreme Court Justice Clark has pointed out, "the history of humankind is inseparable from the history of religion." Even in their most despondent, hopeless moments, our enslaved black brothers and sisters were heard to sing, "If anybody asks you who I am, tell them I'm a child of God." Glorification is but an inspired and spontaneous response to that sense of identity.

As a family physician, it has been apparent to me that the truth for which we search is as close as self. Belief systems are not abstract and esoteric, but are an integral part of behavior and mood. Once again, if our hope and prayer is found in Irving Berlin's hymn "God Bless America," concern for the collective conscience of this great nation must be part of the therapeutic mix.

Section Six

Prognostic Variables and the Benefits of Care

Chapter XXI

The Domestic and Global Benefits of Wholeness Rediscovered

I suspect that much of the floundering described in the last half century was the social expression of confusion—frail families, rising adult and juvenile crime rates, greed and litigiousness, hedonistic sexual misbehavior, public school deterioration, interfaith squabbling, substance abuse, deterioration of international respect, and the consequent social anxiety, depression, and sense of overwhelming stress. We can only hope that a rediscovery of identity and purpose would place a great nation back on course toward the pursuit of even loftier greatness. The domestic rediscovery of identity and wholeness must precede the global appreciation of it.

For those who might say that I am making a big deal out of commonplace sociologic phenomena, I am reminded of a humorous story that circulates within the medical community of the patient who sought medical attention for a bizarre, complex multiplicity of complaints. After a careful history and physical examination, his physician suggested that the condition sounded very much like an acute case of SLAG.

"Gosh, Doctor, what in the world is that?" asked the patient.

"Well", explained the physician, "it's really a mixture of syphilis, Legionnaires' disease, AIDS, and gonorrhea, probably all picked up at the same place."

"That's terrible," responded the patient, "Can anything be done?"

"Yes, the nurse has already reserved a hospital room and I have ordered your diet."

"Diet? What kind of a diet?"

"Well, it basically consists of pancakes and flounder," explained the doctor.

"Gosh, Doc, how can that help?" was the logical response.

"Unfortunately, it doesn't help, but it's the only thing we can slide under the door!"

I only digress to tell that story in an effort to assure the reader that the United States has not reached the pancake and flounder stage of faltering health. I am of the opinion, however, that recovery from the "slippery slope" from greatness is best accomplished when detected early on. For all maladies affecting humankind, early diagnosis is the variable that most affects successful outcome. One of Christ's best-known parables relates to the prodigal son, who demanded his portion of the estate and ran off to spend it on riotous living. If the past sixty years have indeed been the rebellious adolescent misbehavior of our republic, we must ask ourselves if we will come to our senses before we fall to the level of "eating with the pigs."

The restoration of our image as a Christian nation is designed to restore an ethic, as a belief system, that will interface with and automatically interact with the collective sociological and emotional phenomena of our citizenry. Images are meaningful to the extent that they produce healthy identity, behavior, and purpose. Every nation has such a spoken or unspoken functioning system, whether it be known as Hindu, Islamic, Buddhist, or socialistic, to name a few. Once again, restoration of this nation's wholeness to accomplish domestic benefits must precede any consideration of global benefits.

With that in mind, it is just a fact that the Christian message is one of powerful love. Although they are often thought of in a secular sense, I have always looked upon voluntarism and philanthropy as practical expressions of that love. And it is interesting to note that those two exercises are alive and well in the United States today. In many societies living under socialism, voluntarily giving of one's self, time, and resources is not even understood. That is the government's responsibility. In the setting of humanism, generosity is a matter accomplished by reason. But in a Christian sense, it is a powerfully motivated exercise in grateful obedience. Regardless of source, the preservation of a republic with small serving government is dependent on the goodness and voluntarism of its citizenry.

Because of my own gratitude for a life of fulfillment, I have enjoyed serving Ursinus College, the Jefferson Medical College, the Chester County Hospital, the Westminster Presbyterian Church of West Chester, and Rotary at fundraising and board of director levels of service. I have been amazed by the phenomenon of philanthropy motivated by wholesome conviction among the affluent as well as people of limited means. Sacrificial giving to those causes in which we believe has become a vital part of our economy and social health. Nevertheless, we are becoming a nation that adores benefits, and the spirit of stewardship is not what it once was.

Beyond philanthropy, however, it is hoped that a restored sense of worth and goodness will be reflected in stronger nuclear families, stronger schools, and a reduction in adult and juvenile crime, sexual misbehavior, substance abuse, and social stress. This is a religious and patriotic call to all in the best interest of the common good.

The message from *The Greatest Generation*, written by Tom Brokaw, suggests that "you can have your cake and eat it, too." Those who lived through the world wars and Great Depression possessed solid values in trying times.

Health care was comparatively primitive, but honor and love for family, God, and nation were solid. We "pledged allegiance to the flag...and to the *republic* for which it stands." I cannot envision pledging allegiance to a flag and the secular socialism for which it stands. Again, what would happen to a nation that was enjoying the best physical health known to humankind if it regained quality of life by attending to its moral integrity?

After four months of convalescence and rehabilitation, my new hip is behaving beautifully. I am able to rejoin my friends on the golf course, weed my flowerbeds, plant my vegetable garden, sing in the spring concert of my retirement community, and attend meetings at Ursinus College and Jefferson Medical College. By addressing my faltering health, quality of life was able to regain momentum.

The provision of quality of life during the golden years has been successfully afforded in recent decades by continuing care retirement communities (CCRCs). Beyond the assistance provided in matters of meals, housekeeping, and health care, the socialization, avocational committee work, recreational opportunities, cultural encounters, and attention to resident wholeness have been priceless for Anne and me. We have even gone back to choral work.

The White Horse Village Singers is a seventy-five-voice group of singers ranging from seventy to ninety-five years of age. Some are professional musicians of bygone years; some are prior participants in choirs and choruses; and some are just going to sing as long as they can. A recent selection performed by the chorus was Leslie Bricusse's "Fill the World With Love," from the movie *Goodbye, Mr. Chips*. The chorus has been commended for a rendition that reflected a "sincere understanding and love of text." I share that text, for it reflects the values of those who were raised during the first half of the twentieth century.

"In the morning of my life I shall look to the sunrise,

At a moment in my life when the world is new,

And the blessing I shall ask is that God will grant me,
To be brave and strong and true...
And to fill the world with love my whole life through.

In the noontime of my life I shall look to the sunshine,
At a moment in my life when the sky is blue,
And the blessing I shall ask will remain unchanging,
To be brave and strong and true...
And to fill the world with love my whole life through.

In the evening of my life I shall look to the sunset,
At a moment in my life when the night is due,
And the question I shall ask, only I can answer,
Was I brave and strong and true?
Did I fill the world with love my whole life through?

As a matter of therapeutic summary, it has been my civic experience that the "child of God" image generates a proactive force that fosters the replacement of embarrassed shame with patriotic pride, adversarialism with trusting neighborliness, and creeping servitude with liberty. This idealistic scenario paints our vision of therapeutic success. Like most goals, it is designed to motivate us to aim high. We will still have the domestic and international problems of today and those unenvisioned of the future. However, as a successful, thriving republic, we will be much more open to the comprehension and resolution of our own problems, as well as those of other nations.

Now, what about the global effects of a reformed United States? In spite of this half century of domestic uncertainty, our young republic is still watched, envied, and emulated by many. Human nature is remarkably similar in most cultures, and the environment that we provide for family security, opportunity, and achievement is still sought by all. Unfortunately, as the only remaining twentieth-century superpower, we must be concerned about the recent increasing amount of hate and distress that has been directed at the United States of America. In view of our historic contributions to world peace, reconstruction, promotion of human rights, alleviation of human suffering, and advocacy for liberty for all, much of that antipathy is unjust. But many complex forces have contributed to that predicament, including terrorism fostered by religious extremism, the international economic crisis relating to fossil fuel, the unfortunate lingering wars, accusations of imperialism by totalitarian despots, a longstanding tribal mentality still existing in many of our developing nations, an ineffective United Nations, and, too often, criticism fostered by Hollywood and our own news media.

But beyond these reasons for hate, it should be noted that Antoine de la Mothe Cadillac, the French colonial governor who founded the city of Detroit in 1799, once observed that "excellence in all fields of endeavor is always rewarded, and excellence is always punished. Rewarded by those who admire it; and punished by those who are envious." The grand experiment that has become the United States of America has been remarkably successful. And as a result, we are paradoxically the object of both admiration and envy. The translation of scriptural liberty to civil liberty by our nation's founders gave rise to a standard of living that is rooted in free-market capitalism. No one explained this better than Margaret Thatcher, who noted "that there's no alternative to capitalism because it's a system that ensures the most prosperity for the most people." Thatcher acknowledged that capitalism is not controllable or even predictable—but neither is human nature: "Since its inception, capitalism has known slumps and recessions, bubble and froth; no one has yet disinvented the business cycle, and probably no one will...[What are] called the 'gales of creative destruction' still roar mightily from time to time. To lament these things is ultimately to lament the bracing blast of freedom itself."

It is for these reasons that domestic reform is essential. The world needs a role model, and we need to be seen as a great nation that celebrates unity, celebrates diversity, and still thrives as a republic living by the rule of law. Our exemplary existence is the first unspoken witness to nations that solve diversity with ethnic cleansing, political disagreement with blind bombings, religious evangelism with forced confession, and leadership change by military coup.

Beyond setting that good example, we must convey to the world our sincere willingness to help any nation rise to that level of fulfillment. Our first offer must be to meet human need wherever it exists. Human kindness is recognized by most who see it, good works speak for themselves, and no religious claims need be made. The offered services could be delivered by U.S. volunteers, and the people-to-people benefit would enrich the whole process.

We could offer to the world an upfront description of who we are—a free people served by a representative government, consequent unlimited opportunity, a large middle class, care for our weakest members, and living in a state of happiness. For those who admire and wish to emulate us, we could then offer an onsite study of their domestic situation and free counseling to foster the development of a republic of their own.

As former Governor Sarah Palin reminds us, "We are still a republic. We are certainly not doomed to fade away. And we have no desire to be an empire. We don't want to colonize other countries or force our ideals on them. But we have been given a unique responsibility: to show the world the meaning and the rewards of freedom. America, as Reagan said, is 'the abiding alternative to tyranny.' We must remain the Shining City on a Hill to all who seek freedom and prosperity. The world will not be more peaceful if we retreat behind our borders; it will in fact be more dangerous and violent. We don't go looking for fights, but we're ready to face them if necessary. If we ever lose faith in our ideals, the world will be a darker place for those who love peace."

So last, but not least, much unjust hate and criticism is relentless, and many world threats go beyond diplomatic attempts. Many human rights violations viciously disregard civilized reasoning. In such situations, and as a last resort, military intervention becomes a matter of necessity. As the remaining twentieth-century superpower, police responsibilities are an unspoken expectation. Whenever that becomes necessary, the world deserves a complete and convincing explanation, as well as an invitation to participate in the rescue efforts. This approach is especially important as emerging nations become new superpowers of the twenty-first and future centuries.

Fortunately, a superpower with an ethically sound sense of wholeness can make the world a safer, happier, and healthier home for all. And that nation must live with the conviction that the power of love is greater than the power of hate. But God help us all if, in that role, the United States of America forgets the source of its greatness.

Chapter XXII

Ultimate Citizenship

In conclusion, your author, as a Christian layman, would like to make an observation relating to health's bottom line. When all assets and liabilities are finally reconciled, what is the factual net value of comprehensive wholeness for any social unit? From the Christian understanding that our Creator God is an omnipotent, omniscient, and omnipresent lover of His creation, there emerges what Francis Collins calls a worldview. History gains new meaning, life assumes new purpose, and reordered values give new understanding to the pursuit of happiness. This new perspective is the consequence of a strange phenomenon best described as dual citizenship.

By focusing on the faltering health of Uncle Sam, this book has intentionally addressed the subject of citizenship in the United States of America. As a physician, I have endeavored to report factually on the Christian forces that have shaped our nation's birth, growth, and development during our first two hundred years, and I have tried to identify facts suggesting the onset of faltering health during the past sixty years. In so doing, I have not been entirely fair to Christianity. I have referred to belief systems as though faith is a rulebook and the living of life a cookbook experience. Christian "image" is also a cold term that even evokes the concept of idolatry.

Volumes have been written to deepen our understanding of such words as "righteousness," "justification," "atonement," "redemption," "propitiation," "salvation," and even "faith." John R. W. Stott tells us that these words, used in the Christian vocabulary, are unique, and for religion imply "a direction of the movement" of God toward His creation. Even without an intellectual confrontation with sophisticated theological definitions such as these, I have seen diverse people, including some with significant cognitive disorders, attracted to and transformed by the healthful and liberating nature of the Christian experience.

To truly understand the symbiotic relationship between our young republic and Christianity—the dependence of our independence—an understanding of the concept of dual citizenship is essential. Specifically, the Christian believes that he or she has a temporal citizenship in a nation and an eternal one in the kingdom of God. The initiative by God through Jesus Christ is the very central belief of the Christian religion and represents the foundation for the here-and-now medical theology discussed in this book.

The Christian regards citizenship in God's kingdom as ultimate; prays regularly that "Thy kingdom come, Thy will be done on earth as it is in heaven"; and brings to his or her temporal, civic patriotism the hope for the goodness of the eternal kingdom. That hope for idealistic temporal goodness is associated with a personal commitment to effort and a scriptural promise of empowerment. Citizens of the greater kingdom discover a strong sense of healthy identity and responsive gratitude. They regard gifts of talent and family as sacred trusts and are effectively motivated to develop them creatively in the worlds of art, vocation, and social service. And by understanding the Creator as a loving Father, they are powerfully moved to better comprehend the interrelatedness of the human family. This ideal and that power are the benefits embodied in the concept of dual citizenship. And for many observers, the evolution of our beloved nation's brief history suggests the beneficial consequences of dual patriotism.

"Temporal" and "eternal" are words that evoke thoughts relating to time—a dimension that I mentioned in this book's preface. Ten years ago my wife and I were entertaining our whole family on Thanksgiving Day. At the dinner table I happened to mention that the year had gone by quickly, and here it was almost Christmas time again. My oldest grandson, Bobby, never at a loss for words, reacted promptly, "No, Granddad, last Christmas was long ago, and this coming Christmas is a whole month away."

I explained to Bobby that when you are young, time seems to go by more slowly, but for older folks the years pass by quickly. After a moment of reflection he wanted to know if I understood why that was so. I confessed to a lack of understanding of that perception, and he explained that a year for him was one out of seven and for me, one out of seventy. Again, from the mouths of babes…!

Almost all of us at White Horse Village look back on our seventy, eighty, ninety, or one hundred years as an interval of seeming brevity. And with that new perspective, we again confront those persistent questions of human nature—"Does life have meaning? Is there an eternal dimension to self, or is life just a transient experience defined by birth and death?"

The ultimate value to be found in the eternal citizenship addressed here is again captured in the Christian shorter catechism previously discussed—"The chief end of man is to glorify God and to enjoy him forever." Glorification, as an embracing way of life, has been offered as the definitive therapy needed by the citizens of our unstable republic. "To enjoy Him forever," however, provides qualitative and temporal assurances that challenge our comprehension.

Pictured here in 2009, the year of our 60th wedding anniversary is our immediate family – four daughters, sons-in-law, and five grandchildren. The picture is included because it represents the generations that prompted the writing of this book. I covet for them the happiness that was mine during the years of the Great Depression. I have seen evolve the sociologic and economic forces responsible for the faltering health of our great nation. It is my sincere hope that my descendents will work to rediscover the spiritual creativity that I could see in my own parents and grandparents. Affluence without wisdom is treacherously risky.

The "pursuit of happiness" has been long recognized as a powerful force in human behavior and is included in our Declaration of Independence as an unalienable right. Our human inclination to regard happiness as sensual pleasure often results in a derangement of values, disappointment, and unhappiness; but for centuries people have testified to the true happiness associated with ultimate citizenship. That mood and those reordered values bring wholesome nourishment to one's temporal citizenship.

And finally, "to enjoy Him forever" reintroduces that incomprehensible dimension of eternity that includes the here and now. Ultimate citizenship provides for us an ultimate sense of worth, peace of mind, reconciliation, liberty, confidence, and happiness; and it is in the context of that "forever" that each of us understands the brevity of a temporal national citizenship.

In effect, we learn from our covenant citizenship in God's kingdom that we have been made free to serve our Creator and His creation. This paradoxical liberation for the purpose of servitude is at the very heart of our nation's twenty-first-century need. Renewed commitment to that understanding will leave no room for the "spiritual demoralization" described by Toynbee or the "decadence of irresponsible freedom" identified by Solzhenitsyn.

I write about "my sweet land of liberty" because I find, in the conception, growth, and development of the great American experiment, an effort to foster a kingdom "on earth as it is in heaven." The United States of America has gotten off to a good start, but recent evidences of greed, adversarialism, and outright crime suggest that we have not learned from history's civilization cycle and may well be doomed to repeat it. As agents of free choice it is within our power to become instruments of His peace or to persist in our travels down the road of vulnerability to bondage.

In an effort to gain a concluding feel for the twenty-first-century health of our nation, I would invite you to return to our Philadelphia 1788 Constitutional Convention and review the words of Benjamin Franklin, when asked what kind of nation had been created by our Constitution's framers. His answer: "A republic, if you can keep it." As readers, you have walked with me through the medical steps of history taking, physical examination, special studies, tentative diagnosis, symptomatic therapy, and definitive cure. The one last step for all of us is the question so often asked by patient, family, and friends—"Doctor, now that you have done as much as you can do, what is your prognosis?"

I consulted with you at the time of tentative diagnosis, and I consult with you now. I have been burned by that prognostic question more than once, for sometimes there were distant hidden spreading cancer cells unknown to me as the attending physician, and the patient was sicker than I thought. And what about the patient? Patient compliance is a major problem for doctors in the matters of health care. Will the patient accept the offered diagnosis and follow the suggested therapeutic advice? All of these variables are factors that affect prognostic predictions.

Within the profession, consultants are often humorously defined as physicians called in to share the blame, and in that spirit, dear reader, I seek your opinion. How sick is the patient we love—where would you place our twenty-first-century USA on our civilization cycle? In reaction to Ben Franklin's implied concern, how close are we to keeping or losing our republic? To what extent have the forces of secular socialism eroded the delicate ideal of liberty? And what are the prospects for the patient with faltering health to even seek recovery?

Your crash course in health care has hopefully helped you understand the shades-of-gray world in which the practicing physician labors each day. A variety of opinions is to be expected, but much will have been accomplished if the exercise gets all of us thinking in the best interest of healthy citizenship in the great nation we love.

Writing this book as a physician, and inviting you to think like one about the "patient USA," has great misleading potential. The book title should prompt each of us to ask, "Who is my Uncle Sam?" In our mind's eye we instinctively conjure up and focus on that nice old-fellow image with top hat and red, white and blue vestments. In truth, as indicated by Benjamin Franklin in 1788, it is our republic to keep. The question directed at Benjamin Franklin at Independence Hall and Ben's answer were personalized, because the keeping or losing of a republic is dependent on the sincere commitment of large numbers of good people. In the fullness of truth we have met the patient, and he is us.

To preserve the sovereignty of the citizenry, a government that serves them, and the liberty that is instinctively coveted by all, goodness is the key to greatness. "Righteousness exalteth a nation" is the scriptural proverb that captures that truth. Good folks look out for each other. On the other hand, liberty is eroded when the love of money, lust for power, pride, greed, and crime produce the need for more law, more bureaucratic regulation, bigger government, and higher taxes. History suggests that secularism and socialism go hand in hand.

Recognizing that collective goodness is intimately related to the healthy cultivation of a collective religious nature, our founding fathers declared our independence in the context of a Creator's kingdom. The complementary dependent relationship was captured by the Reverend Samuel Francis Smith in 1831 when he penned:

Our Father's God, to thee,

Author of liberty,

To Thee we sing.

Long may our land be bright

With freedom's holy light

Protect us by thy might,

Great God, our King.

This fourth verse of Reverend Smith's hymn, titled "America," succinctly identifies a nation within a kingdom that is ruled by a God who graciously provides liberty, freedom, and protection. It is of interest that the hymn was written for music used for a century by England as a national anthem. That being so, we are reminded of humankind's struggle for dignity and liberty—from the sovereignty of a deified royal family to the Magna Carta to the concept of parliament to a Declaration of Independence embodying the self-evident truth that all people are created equal.

A citizenry that is sovereign and an elected government that is servile are experiments that are still in process. We must periodically stop and remember how this came to be. Let us hope that each generation will do its part to foster the goodness upon which greatness is dependent. That hope was captured by Katherine Lee Bates when she wrote:

O beautiful for patriot dream

That sees beyond the years.

Thine alabaster cities gleam,

Undimmed by human tears!

America! America!

God shed his grace on thee,

And crown thy good with brotherhood

From sea to shining sea!

In concert with the beliefs of Arnold Toynbee, I am of the opinion that apathy, weakness, vulnerability, and a return to bondage need not be the inevitable fate of all cultures and civilizations. I truly believe that an affluent and greedy populace can come to its senses, recover from its spiritual demoralization, and reset its sails in the best interest of goodness, greatness, and survival. It is possible to "have your cake and eat it, too." Applying the human mind to the prolongation of life, developing technologies that are not yet envisioned, and creating a fine quality of life for all can contribute to that "patriotic dream" as long as we humbly acknowledge the brilliance and grace of the Creator, who authored it all.

Bibliography

Preface

- Webster—*Webster's Ninth New Collegiate Dictionary*, 1989, Merriam-Webster Press.

Chapter I

- Baer, John—*The Pledge of Allegiance, a Revised History and Analysis*, 2007. Annapolis, MD Free State Press, Inc. 2007.
- Bates, Katherine Lee—"America the Beautiful," 1893. *The Presbyterian Hymnal*, Westminster John Knox Press 1990.
- Boyd, Julian P.—*The Declaration of Independence, The Evolution of the Text*, The Library of Congress in association with the Thomas Jefferson Memorial Foundation, Inc., University Press of New England, 1999.
- Logan, General John A.—"The History of Memorial Day"; Internet http://www.history.com/ministte.do?
- Sandberg, Carl—*Abraham Lincoln: Volume I, The Prairie Years*, Chapter 10. Harcourt, Brace, and Company, Inc. 1926.
- Schor, Esther—Emma Lazarus, "The New Colossus," Princeton University, 1883.

Chapter II

- Internet, http://allabouthistory.org/in-god-we-trust.htm, All About History—In God We Trust.
- Poole, Robert III, M.D.—"The Evolution of Health Care in the Community of West Chester, PA, 1799-1999."
- Rodebaugh, Paul A.—*West Chester, The First 200 Years: 1799-1999, A Bicentennial Souvenir*, edited by Paul A. Rodebaugh, Jeffrey Rollison, and Eric Chandlee Wilson, 1999, published by the Borough of West Chester.

- Wagner, Frederick B., Jr., M.D.—Thomas Jefferson University Lea and Ferbiger, 1989.

Chapter III

- ACLU—American Civil Liberties Union—Wikipedia, http://en.wikipedia.org/wiki/american-civil-liberties.
- Clinton, William—Impeachment of Bill Clinton, Wikipedia, http://wikipedia.org/wiki/impeachment-of-bill-clinton
- *Daily Local News*—Friday, February 27, 2008, "More Than One in Every One Hundred U.S. Adults in Prison."
- Foote, Donna—"A Year With Teach for America," *Newsweek*, August 11, 2008, page 47.
- Gross, Donna—"The Economy, Why It's Worse Than You Think," *Newsweek*, June 11, 2008, page 21.
- Jefferson, David—"The Divorced Generation Grows Up," *Newsweek*, April 21, 2008, page 47.
- Matthews, Jay—"America's Top High Schools," 2008 Small Schools Rising, *Newsweek*, May 26, 2008, page 42.
- Miller, Jennifer—"The Final Step in Home Defense; Learning When and How to Use Guns," *Daily Local News*, Tuesday, November 25, 2008.

Chapter IV

- Collins, Francis S.—*The Language of God*, Free Press, 2006.
- Dittmar, Mary Jane—"Making a Difference: The FDA and Natural Substances Approval," *Better Nutrition*, February 1990.
- Pritchett, Henry S.—*Abraham Flexner, A Biography*, Columbia University Press, New York, 1943.

Chapter V

- Socrates—"Know Thyself," Internet www.spaceandemotion.com/philosophy. Socrates.philosopher.htm.

Chapter VI

- Kelfer, Russell ©—*You are Who You Are for a Reason, www.dtm.org* ©
- Russell, Bertrand—*Why I am Not a Christian*, Simon & Schuster, Inc., New York, 1957.
- Warren, Rev. Rick—*The Purpose Driven Life*, 2002, Zondervan, Grand Rapids, Michigan.

Chapter VII

- Bible—The Old Testament Book of Micah.
- Harris, Paul P.—My Road to Rotary, 1948 Rotary International, Evanston, IL.

Chapter VIII

- Beeman, Richard R., Ph.D.—"A Republic, If You Can Keep It," The National Constitution Center, April 1, 2008.
- Collins, Rev. Kenneth W.—Russia, Christian Nation Internet www.kencollins.com/poll-05.htm, copyright 1995-2008, by the Rev. Kenneth W. Collins. Reprinted with permission.
- Gorski, Eric—"Religion in Flux," by Eric Gorski, Associated Press Religion Writer, *The Daily Local News*, Friday February 29, 2008.
- Waldman, Steven—"Golly Madison," The Founding Faith, published in *Newsweek* March 17, 2008.

Chapter IX

- Toynbee, Arnold—*A Study of History*, Oxford University Press and Thames and Hudson, Ltd.

Chapter X

- Bacon, Francis—*The Essays or Counsels, Civil and Moral of Francis Bacon*, Published by McClurg, 1900, Chicago.
- Quindlen, Anna—"Living History," published in *Newsweek*, November 17, 2008, page 123.

- Yost, Calvin D., Ph.D.—*Ursinus College—A History of the First One Hundred Years*, published by Ursinus College, 1985.

Chapter XI

- Lithwick, Dahlia—"The High Court, a Users Guide," *Newsweek*, June 30, 2008, page 31.
- Supreme Court—83 Supreme Court Reporter-374 US 203, page 1560, "The Opinion of the Court delivered by Mr. Justice Clark."
- Taylor, Steven—"Politicians on the Bench," *Newsweek*, July 14, 2008, page 46.

Chapter XII

- Bible—New Testament Book of James.
- Polio Plus, *The Rotarian* magazine.

Chapter XIII

- Hauser, Marc D., Ph.D.—"Is Morality Natural?" *Newsweek*, September 22, 2008, page 65.
- Phillips, J. B.—*Your God is Too Small*, 1997, Touchstone (registered trademark of Simon & Schuster, Inc.), New York, NY.
- Sendler, Irena—Obituary—*The Economist*, May 24, 2008.
- Van Biema, David—"Mother Teresa's Crisis of Faith," *Time* magazine;
- cover title—"The Secret Life of Mother Teresa," September 3 or August 23, 2007.
- Toynbee, Arnold—*A Study of History,* Chapter IV, "The Breakdown of Civilizations." Revised and Abridged Edition of Barnes and Noble, Inc., 1995.

Chapter XIV

- Brown, Kevin—*Alexander Fleming: The Man and the Myth*, Oxford University Press, Oxford, 1984.

- Porter, Roy—*The Cambridge Illustrated History of Medicine,* Cambridge University Press, Cambridge, England, 1996.
- Wagner, Frederick B., Jr., M.D.—Thomas Jefferson University Lea and Febiger 1989.

Chapter XV

- Alter, Jonathan, "Bill Gates Goes to School," *Newsweek,* December 15, 2008, page 42.
- American Psychiatric Association Diagnostic and Statistical Manual of Mental Disorders DSM—IV—TRtm—Sexual and Gender Identity Disorders, page 535.
- Bible—New Testament, Matthew Chapters 5-7.
- Brandon, Lawrence G., *Pathway to Progress,* CPCU-Loman Education Foundation, 2003.
- Clark, Supreme Court Justice—83 Supreme Court Reporter—347 US 203 The Opinion of the Court as delivered by Mr. Justice Clark.
- *Daily Local News*—Monday, August 4, 2008, "Famed Author Alexander Solzhenitsyn Dies," Moscow Associated Press.
- Daschle, Sen. Tom—*What We Can Do About The Health Care Crisis,* Thomas Dunne Books, St. Martins Press, 2008.
- Foote, Donna—"A Year With Teach for America," *Newsweek,* August 11, 2008, page 47.
- Howard, Philip K., Esq.—*The Death of Common Sense,* published by Warner Books, Inc., 1994.
- Jefferson, David J.— "The Divorce Generation Grows Up," *Newsweek,* April 21, 2008, page 47.
- Kennedy, John F.—Inaugural Address, January 20, 1961, *Inaugural Addresses of Presidents of the United States,* Washington, D.C., January 2001, Bartleby (publisher). Authors: U.S. Congress and Joint Congressional Committee on Inaugural Ceremonies.

- Miller, Lisa—"The Religious Call for Gay Marriage," *Newsweek,* December 15, 2008, page 28.

- Seckel, Al—*Bertrand Russell On God and Religion,* edited by publisher Prometheus Books; 1986.

- Schaff, Philip—*History of the Christian Church*, 1910, Charles Scribner's Sons.

- Thomas, Cal—"Slozhenitsyn's Prophecy for America," *Daily Local News*, August 8, 2008.

- Toynbee, Arnold—*A Study of History*, Oxford University Press and Thames and Hudson, Ltd.

- Waite, Linda J., and Maggie Gallagher—*The Case for Marriage*, New York, Doubleday, 2000.

- Wallerstern, Judith S., Julia M. Lewis, Sandra Blakeslee, *The Unexpected Legacy of Divorce*, New York, Hyperion, 2000.

Chapter XVI

- Bernet, William, M.D. – *Gender Identity Disorder Psychiatry—Current Diagnosis and Treatment*; Second Edition—Ebert, Loosen, Nurcombe, Lechman; McGraw Hill Lange.

- Clark, Supreme Court Justice—83 Supreme Court Reporter—347 US 203 The Opinion of the Court Delivered by Mr. Justice Clark.

- Einstein, Albert—*Relativity: The Special and General Theory*, 1920 H. Holt and Company, New York.

- Free Thought—Free Thought Society of Greater Philadelphia, Internet http://www.FSGP.org/.

- Howard, Philip K., Esq.—*The Death of Common Sense*, Warner Books Inc., 1994.

- *Collapse of the Common Good,* The Ballentine Publishing Group, 2001.

- Samuelson, Robert J., "Lobbying is Democracy in Action," *Newsweek*, December 22, 2008, page 29.

- Schwartz, Bernard—*The Ascent of Pragmatism: The Burger Court in Action,* Addison-Wesley Publishing Company, Reading, MA, 1990.
- Socrates—"Know Thyself," Internet //www.spaceandmotion.com/ Philosophy-Socrates-Philosopher.htm.
- Surrick, Robert B., Esq.—Lawyers, Judges and Journalists—The Corrupt and the Corruptors, 2003
- Will, George—"Freedoms Endangered by Lawsuits," *Daily Local News* January 11, 2009.

Chapter XVII

- Beeman, Richard R.—"A Republic If You Can Keep It," National Constitution Center, April 1, 2008.
- Congressional Budget Office—*Long Range Fiscal Policy Brief—July 3, 2002. A 125 Year Picture of the Federal Government's Share of the Economy, 1950–2075.*
- Freedman, Michael—"Big Government is Back—Big Time," *Newsweek*, February 16, 2009, p. 24.
- Levy, Steven—"Bill Gates' Goodbye to Microsoft," *Newsweek*, June 30, 2008.
- Norquist, Grover. "Happy Cost of Government Day"—FoxNews. com, August 11, 2009.
- Stossel, John—"The Entitlement Mess Needs a Solution," *Daily Local News*, June 18, 2008.
- Stossel, John—"Government Promises are Merely Lies," *Daily Local News*, January 9, 2009.
- Thomas, Cal—"Solzhenitsyn's Prophecy for America," *Daily Local News*, August 8, 2008.
- Will, George—"Data Reveals Conservatives More Giving," *Daily Local News*, March 27, 2008.

Chapter XVIII

- Berlin, Irving—"God Bless America," Library of Congress (original version written in 1918, but modified in 1938 to the piece we know today), 1938.
- Bevilacqua, Cardinal Anthony—"Anthony Bevilacqua," Wikipedia, the Free Encyclopedia, November 19, 2008, 20:48 UTC.
- Bible—The New Testament, Matthew Chapter 22; the New Testament, Romans Chapter 7; Westminster Study Edition, Westminster Press, Philadelphia.
- Bober, Mandell Morton—*Karl Marx's Interpretation of History*, Harvard University Press, Cambridge, MA, 1950.
- Catechism—The Westminster Shorter Catechism, General Assembly of the Orthodox Presbyterian Church, 1978 (from the original in 1647).
- Emmons, Robert A., Ph.D.—"Science Discovers the Secret to Happiness," August 2, 2008, *Bottom Line Retirement*, Volume 8.
- Faber, Frederick William—"There's a Wideness in God's Mercy," 1854, The Presbyterian Hymnal, 1990.
- Gerson, Michael—"The Gospel of Chaplain John," *Newsweek* magazine, September, 8, 2008, page 62.
- Seckel, Al—*Bertrand Russell on God and Religion*, Prometheus Books, 1986
- Renoux, Christian, Ph.D.—Prayer of St. Francis, printed in 1912 by a French religious magazine called La Clochette Paris, Editions Franiscaines 2001.
- Thomas, Cal—"Solzhenitsyn's Prophecy for America," *Daily Local News*, August 8, 2008.
- Toynbee, Arnold—*A Study of History*, Oxford University Press.
- Westminster Presbyterian Church of West Chester, PA—Church Bulletin of Sunday April 13, 2008.

- Will, George—"Debating the Issue of Crime Rates," *Daily Local News*, June 22, 2008.

Chapter XIX

- Seckel, Al—*Bertrand Russell on God and Religion*, Edited by Publisher Prometheus Books, 1986.
- Toynbee, Arnold—*A Study of History*, Oxford University Press.

Chapter XX

- Brannan, Heather, M.D.—"The History of Smallpox: The Rise and Fall of a Disease," *New York Times* Company, September 24, 2004.
- Clark, Supreme Court Justice—83 Supreme Court Reporter—347 US 203 The Opinion of the Court.
- McGann, Mary E.—"If Anybody Asks You Who I Am," *A Precious Fountain* by Mary E. McGann, 2004, Liturgical Press Collegeville, MN.
- Young, The Rev. Robert D., Ph.D.—"The Transition Years, 1989–1994," Westminster Presbyterian Church, 2008.

Chapter XXI

- Bible—New Testament, I Corinthians Chapter 13.
- Brokaw, Tom—*The Greatest Generation*, Random House, Inc., 1998.
- *Fill the World With Love* (from "Goodbye, Mr. Chips"), words and music by Leslie Bricusse, Copyright © 1968, 1969 METRO-GOLDWYN-MAYER, Inc, EMI Hastings Catalog, Inc (Publishing) and Alfred Publishing Company (Print), Inc, Los Angeles, CA, all rights reserved; used by permission.
- Palin, Sarah—*Going Rogue.* Harper Collins Publishers, 2009, pp. 360 & 394.
- Pico, Robert—*Cadillac, The Man Who Founded Detroit,* Paris Denoel, 1995.

- Stott, John R. W.—*The Message of Romans*, Intervarsity Press, England, 1994.
- Zakaria, et al,—"Five Ways to Save the World," by Zakaria, Bloomberg, Alter, Gross, and Begley, *Newsweek*, September 29, 2008, page 45.

Chapter XXII

- Bates, Kathryn Lee—"America the Beautiful," 1893, The Presbyterian Hymnal, Westminster John Knox Press, 1990.
- Bible—Old Testament, Proverbs Chapter 14; New Testament, Matthew Chapters 5, 6, and 13.
- Smith, Samuel Francis—"America," The Christian History Institute, Internet http:chi.gospelcom.net/dallyf/2001/07/daily-7-04-2001.shtml.